SHE
SUFFERED
IN SILENCE

TRULY FAITHFUL II

SHE SUFFERED IN SILENCE

iUniverse books may be ordered through booksellers or by contacting:

iUniverse
1663 Liberty Drive
Bloomington, IN 47403
www.iuniverse.com
1-800-Authors (1-800-288-4677)

Because of the dynamic nature of the Internet, any web addresses or links contained in this book may have changed since publication and may no longer be valid. The views expressed in this work are solely those of the author and do not necessarily reflect the views of the publisher, and the publisher hereby disclaims any responsibility for them.

Any people depicted in stock imagery provided by Thinkstock are models, and such images are being used for illustrative purposes only. Certain stock imagery © Thinkstock.

ISBN: 978-1-4917-7659-9 (sc)
ISBN: 978-1-4917-7658-2 (e)

Library of Congress Control Number: 2015914347

Print information available on the last page.

iUniverse rev. date: 02/29/2016

INTRODUCTION

This book is to help young mothers, parents to be aware that children especially girls are molested and raped in the home as well as outside the home by their own family members. Young woman should have enough respect for themselves not to let anyone use their body for a few minutes of pleasure. It will cost you a whole lifetime of pain. Say no to sex and yes to marriage.

Adrienne's life from a child to an adult, she was molested as a child and later on raped as a teenager, and as an adult. Life is not safe nor is it easy for children or adults. But she thanked God she's still here to sing and give Him Praise for His goodness. She realized she could have been dead and gone, but God has a plan for her life. It was a blessing for her to be able to write this book. She thanked God for keeping her through it all. God blessed her to write this book as an example and inspiration to other young women everywhere. Because she didn't know the Lord for herself, she made a lot of mistakes and wrong choices in her life. Adrienne went about doing what she thought was right, looking for love in all the wrong places, trying to find peace for her soul, but she was running so fast, she ran right into evil everywhere she went. She would like to encourage you to seek God first in your life, and He will direct your past. Call on the name of Jesus our Lord and Savior. The way to seek Him is to read and study the bible daily, starting with the Ten Commandments, the book of Proverbs tells us how we should live, and not live. The Bible is our everyday instructions. If we listen to what God is telling us to do. God is calling us to Repentance and Obedience. Then why do you keep doing things your way. Get to know God for yourself. Mothers and fathers, teach your children the ways of God. Proverbs 22: 6 tells us to train up a child in the way he should go and when he is old, he will not depart from it. Isaiah 54:13 says, and all thy children shall be taught of the Lord; and great shall be the peace of thy children. The word tells us that we are born into a world of sin, but God does not intent for us to stay in sin. He is giving us a choice and a chance to get it right so that we may have eternal life with Him forever. A child should never have to go through sexual abuse of any kind in their life. It exists more often than not. It is the parent job to teach and protect their children by teaching them to speak up and speak out against the evil ones. Teach them that it's all right to say No, so they want make wrong choices in their life.

Ladies we have to be careful whom we leave our children with. Or whom we bring into our home over our children. Evil is everywhere. There are all kinds of people in this world. Children are being molested or killed everyday at the hands of a friend, stranger, boyfriend, uncle, cousin, father, brother, the list goes on. God said to trust no man. Man will continue to molest children as long as he or she can get away with it. If a person molests you, more than likely, he has and will molest someone else. The cycle continues unless they are stopped. The enemy wants to steal, kill, and destroy us, because of the plan God has for our lives. The devil wants to destroy our children to keep them from getting to where God wants them to be. Adrienne found the Lord for herself. What she didn't know was, through it all, He was keeping her. It's all a test to see where your faith lies. In God the Father and His Son Jesus or in man.

Glory Be To God!

CHAPTER ONE

It was Christmas time and everything was quiet. It was cold and dark with snow on the ground outside. Adrienne remembered feeling afraid, and alone, but there was a house full of people. She really didn't know who they all were, but something seems strange. Being the innocent little girl she was, her nightmares had just begun. As she thought to herself, who were all of these strange people she didn't know? Her first thought of being alive here on this earth, was when she was combing her mother's hair.

Adrienne's mother liked having her comb her hair as she sat on the back of a chair that sat against the wall behind her, scratching her scalp pretending to be a hair stylist. It was Christmas Eve, and there was talk that Santa Claus would soon be there. Adrienne heard a loud thump on the roof, so she ran and jumped in the bed. The house was dark and they didn't have electricity the way they do today, they used lanterns, and had out houses, wood stoves and fireplaces. Adrienne remembered her mother having a small Charlie Brown looking tree that had different color sugar candies stuck on it for a Christmas tree, and when Christmas was over, her mother would let them eat the candy from the tree. Then sadly one day her mother wasn't there anymore. She remembered hearing someone say her mother had been taken to the hospital. Adrienne didn't know what a hospital was at the time because of her age, but she kept waiting for her mother to return from the hospital, but she never saw her mother alive again. She remembered her mother looked so beautiful lying there in her pink or was it a blue dress as though she was sleeping. She remembered her sister, brother and herself sitting their quietly in front of their mother. Adrienne waited for her to wake up, but she didn't. It took a long time for Adrienne to realize her mother wasn't coming home again, that she was with God now, high up in the sky. It was a sad time for Adrienne, but she was too young to understand all the things that were changing so fast around her. That was when depression sat in, because nothing was the same after her mother passed away. Things were constantly changing as quickly as you can blink an eye. The darkness got even darker since no one bothered to explain to her about her mother, what death was, or why her mother had to go away? Adrienne didn't know how to explain what she was feeling or the reason why she was feeling the way she did. All she could think was when was her mother coming back to get her and why did she have to leave her? As a shy little girl, Adrienne was afraid and felt so alone. Some memories of her mother was a blessing even though they were just a few memories, it troubled her that she didn't get to know her mother a little while longer before God called her home to be with Him. It also troubled her that no one bothered to take the time to explain to her about death, and that her mother wasn't coming back. She waited for her mother each day that went by, and she never came. Shortly after her mother went away, she remembered it was very dark outside. They didn't have outside lights, and a car pulled up to the house where they were, and inside the car was a man, he started putting something in the trunk of the car, which turned out to be bags of clothes. There was her sister, brother, and herself that went along on the ride. She later learned that the man was there dad, whom she didn't know personally. Her parents must not have been together at that time, the reason why she didn't know her dad. Adrienne's mother was with a man that had eight children, and she had three children of her own. That must have been who all those other people were, in the house. The stress of that many children, Adrienne imagined was a little much for her mother, with her mother having an enlarged heart and all, she found out some years later. Adrienne's dad married a woman with four children of her own, two girls and two boys. Her dad left his family for another family, maybe that was the reason Adrienne didn't know her dad, or was it that she was too young to know who he was. Anyway, the ride was so long that she fell asleep, only to awake in a place she had no idea where they were or why? The car stopped in front of a house where there were other children and a woman there, they were put right to bed after arriving at the house. Adrienne didn't remember being told who this woman was, but by her being the baby of the three children, she didn't understand what was going on, but she knew something wasn't right, this was not her home anymore, and that was not her bed. When she awoke the next morning, there was no one in the house but her, the woman, and a small baby. She thought she was having a bad dream. It was as though she had fallen asleep and woke up in hell. She could only wish things would go back to the way they were before her mother passed away. Her dad had gone off to work early that morning before she was up out of bed, he left her there with this strange woman, and the beat her in a way she had never experienced before. Adrienne was five years old, because she was just starting to realize that she was a person. Adrienne remembered being in school before moving to this place, but after moving, she wasn't allowed to go to school, because she had to be six years old before a sudden time of the year. All Adrienne could think about was why did this woman hate her so much? It was like she had stepped into a dream, and couldn't get out no matter how hard she tried waking up. Adrienne had an uneasy feeling inside about the woman, and she was right. The abuse started that very same day for Adrienne, shaking with fear, she was so afraid she wet the bed. The woman her stepmother abused her in a way she had never been abused before, whatever that was the woman had given her to eat for breakfast made her sick to her stomach, so sick that she threw it up. The woman hit her so hard upside the head that it knocked her from the kitchen table to the floor. Adrienne lay there on the floor crying, wondering to herself why this woman would do this to her? The other children had gone off to school. Adrienne was not old enough to attend school yet, but she remembered being in the first grade at Malibu High School before moving to Jackson. She had to wait until she was six before she could attend first the grade which left her all along in the house with this woman who was a stranger to her, so was the baby. Adrienne couldn't remember her dad introducing her to this woman as her stepmother so it told a little while for her to understand who this woman was. Her dad was always away working, so she never got to see much of him, he was a stranger to her as well, when Adrienne got up in the mornings, her dad was already gone to work. Whenever she went to bed at night her dad still wouldn't have come in from work yet or just hadn't made it home until after she was already in bed. Adrienne dad Marcus worked on the railroad and it kept him away from home a lot. Only for him to get home after all the children had already gone to bed, or was it that she stayed in the back room to stay out of the way of her stepmother, and she didn't know her dad was at home. Some nights her dad never came home at all, whenever his job would send him out of town during a derailment and sometime he was only home on the weekend. All the children had there our chores to do, and they had to be done before bedtime, which was eight o'clock on the dot. They could only iron their clothes on the weekend, and they had to wear their clothes two days in a row after changing their clothes when they got home from school each day, before putting them in the dirty clothes basket. Adrienne didn't even know who her dad was until she was a teenager. She would hear his voice some days, but she didn't get to see his face because he sounded so angry all the time. Adrienne remembered staying to herself a lot. Adrienne didn't speak a whole lot after her mother passed away, and nobody noted how lonely she was without her mother. Adrienne thought she was just in the way of everyone else, and afraid her dad Marcus, would see the bruises on her body, and at the same time she was afraid of what her stepmother Hanna, was gonna do to her the next day. Adrienne didn't realize, had she showed her dad the bruises, things would have been different in her life. For some reason Adrienne always put other people feelings before her own, which made her angry and sad, or was that fear too. Adrienne had no idea of how to defend herself from Hanna her stepmother without being just like she was, mean and hateful, it just wasn't in her. If only she had known then to pray. She was a child, and not a bad child, but was treated badly. Adrienne was blamed for everything that happened by Hanna, her stepmother's children, and Hanna would punish Adrienne, asking her no questions about the situation. For some reason Hanna always had it in for Adrienne, it was something everyday, a reason for Hanna to punish Adrienne. Hanna would look for a reason to beat Adrienne, from combing her hair, and Hanna knew Adrienne was tender headed, but she didn't care, Hanna would give Adrienne a bath, just so she could hold her head under the water, as she struggled to get free. Adrienne knew she wasn't a bad child, just was treated badly. She was too afraid to be bad. Adrienne stayed in the backroom after all of the other children had gone off to school, trying to stay out the way of her stepmother. But Hanna always knew just where to find her, looking for a reason to do whatever she wanted to her while no one else was around to stop her. Adrienne started wetting the bed, this was something which she had no control over, it just happened while she was asleep. She couldn't remember ever wetting the bed before thins began to change in her life. Hanna would sometimes tire Adrienne down to the bed with no clothes on and just beat her until she got tired. There were times that she would place Adrienne head in between her legs to where she couldn't move, and all she could do was hollow and cry, but no one could hear her screaming. Adrienne didn't know to ask God to help her. There were times Hanna would put her foot on Adrienne's head pressing it to the floor as she beat her with an extension cord, she was so afraid of this woman, that she stayed in the back room away from everyone else. Adrienne felt so sad and embarrassed that Hanna would do this to her. She had no idea what to do. She had no one she could talk to about it, since she didn't know anyone to tell, living in a strange place, everything was hard for her to grasp, being afraid all the time. The abuse went on well into her teenage years. Through it all, Adrienne tried to remain humble. She was sad and hurt that evil was all around her. She was a victim of child abuse, all of her young life. Fear kept her from telling anyone, or was it her stepmother, Hanna. Adrienne remembered Hanna saying to her that whatever went on in that house was to stay in that house. Adrienne knew it was God that kept her sane when she thought she was losing her mind. Adrienne remembered having a little doll that she had named little Squeegee because she was so soft. Adrienne couldn't remember where she had gotten little Squeegee or what had happened to her, but she would talk to her as though she was a person just to have someone that she could talk to, even though she couldn't help her or talk back to her. Still Adrienne didn't understand or know God and His son Jesus, because they were not talked about in the house, but she had this feeling that someone was watching her all the time. She had no idea that it was God watching over her, but she could feel His presence.

The days were long, and the abuse even worse, not only was Adrienne being abused by Hanna her stepmother, but was being sexually abused by Hanna's son, Billy as well. Adrienne's dad and Hanna had together six children. Adrienne's dad had three children. Hanna had four children, two boys and two girls. Before they got married. One of the girls was given away and raised by a family member when she was born. Adrienne thought, Hanna had the child at a young age, and gave the child to a family member that couldn't have children. A total of eleven children in the house, the twelfth one died. Billy only did to Adrienne what her dad did to his stepdaughter Rhonda, before she was send to live with the same people who was raising Hanna's other child. Adrienne finally realized why Hanna hated her so much, and she didn't mine showing Adrienne just how much she hated her. As Adrienne grew older her dad would always tell her she looked just like her mother, and that just really sat Hanna off and she would take it out on Adrienne when her dad Marcus wasn't around. Adrienne was the baby of Marcus three children, so she always got the worse end of everything, hand me down clothes, shoes, sometime she went to school without pencil or paper because

She didn't want to have to ask Hanna for them. Adrienne needed glasses, but was too afraid to ask for anything, after the way she was being treated. All of the hollowing, and fighting, Adrienne was a nervous wreck. Adrienne tried to keep herself busy around the house doing whatever she saw needed to be done. In order to keep down the hollowing and the beatings, but it seemed the more she did, the more she had to do, having to wash dishes before she was big enough to reach the dish pan. Adrienne had to stand on a box in order to reach the pan to wash the dishes, there were no sinks like we have today. Having to carry wood for the fireplace, working in the gardens from sun up to sun down sometimes, drawing water from the well, she had to feed the chickens on the yard, or gather the eggs at her grandmother's house, sweeping off the yard, watch clothes by hand and hang them on the fence in the cold, sometime the snow, cooking and cleaning the house, picking up paper off the yard, there was something to do all the time. Her dad said, this would keep them out of jail, because if one of them went to jail, not to call him. Adrienne brother ended up going to prison anyway for stealing a dress out of the window of a department store for Hanna.

Adrienne believed Hanna put him up to it. Hanna did all she could to get reed of Adrienne and her dad other two children. She remembered Hanna would burn her on purpose, with the straightening comb when she would press her hair and Adrienne better not have said anything, or she would have got popped in the head with the straightening comb. Adrienne had this imaginary friend that she would talk to, she always felt this presents around her, but there was no one there, Adrienne didn't know at the time, that God had sent His angels to watch over her, as He was carrying her through it all, waiting for her to ask for His help.

Adrienne didn't have a clue she was suppose to ask God for his help. Had she known her life would of been different, but then she realized that if she hadn't gone through all that she went through, then she wouldn't have know God for herself. Adrienne stayed to herself a lot in hopes that someday it would all be over, and she wouldn't have to live that way always. Adrienne read somewhere trouble doesn't last always, and what do you know, God's word is true. God the Father and His son Jesus Christ wasn't taught or talked about in the house, she knew of them from going to Sunday school, and from what she learned from her grandmother. God bless her soul as she would listen to her grandmother sing, pray, and read her bible every time she was around her, and that's been every since she was old enough to know who her grandmother was, but yet she didn't understand it all. She would tell them to take the Lord along with them everywhere they went. Her grandmother would pray for all of her children, and their children, and their children's children. Adrienne grandmother for as long as she could remember had prayer meeting on Saturday and Sunday nights and sometime during the week or just whenever, and if you were there in her house you had to join in, she made sure of that. All the adults had their turn to sing a song and then pray, and the children would have to say the Lord's Prayer together, that was how Adrienne learned to say the Lord's Prayer, and she made it her every day prayer until she was an adult. Adrienne found that it wasn't enough just to say the Lord's Prayer.

She needed to have her own personal relationship with God through prayer. In doing so the devil got busy trying to destroy her through other people, which was what the devil was doing all alone, trying to kill her. Things got so bad Adrienne was at the point of taking her own life by taking a hand full of pills. She just wanted to fall asleep never to wake up to this world again. Little did she know that that was what the devil wanted her to do, kill herself, then he would sit back and laugh at her, and she would have been one more soul going straight to hell alone with him.

On Sunday mornings all the children had to walk for miles to get to Church, they had to walk through the woods, over and under bob wire fence, across two lanes of interstate highway, and then walk back to the house, when there was a car sitting in the yard. Adrienne's mind was so focused on the bad things that were happening to her, she couldn't remember any good times in her life growing up. She wanted to be happy, but she didn't know how. Because of all the abuse she suffered, the devil played tricks with her mind, keeping her mind on all the abuse she suffered instead of what was important, which was God.

Adrienne was experiencing abuse in every way possible, and it made her so angry inside, but was too afraid to act out on it. Adrienne was angry that man could be so hateful to her. Not only was she physically and sexually abused, but emotionally and verbally as well. She had no knowledge of good and evil, but could feel what was happening to her was wrong, that's why she was feeling angry, hurt, sad, and alone all at the same time. Being molested by a family member, she couldn't remember how old she was when the molestation started, but remember being awaken from a deep sleep one night with him on top of her, she didn't understand what was happening to her, but she somehow knew that it was wrong. Not only was she being molested, there was four girls in one bed. Adrienne hated what she was going through; she just didn't have the courage to put a stop to it at the time. She realized that it was fear that kept her from telling anyone, she was afraid of what would happen to her if she told. She wished she had known to call on the Lord, right then. Adrienne one day got up the courage to confront the person that molested her and threatened to tell someone if he didn't stop sneaking into the girl's room. All of the girl's slept in one room, and all the boys in another room just down the hall of each other, and he would sneak into the girl's room at night after he thought everyone was asleep as he ignored her warning and thought he would try it again the next night but this time Adrienne was waiting for him as he eased around the bed and begin to pull back the covers to climb on her, but her foot met him as she kicked him as hard as she could to keep him off of her, in a place only he and God knows where she kicked him. Adrienne couldn't stand the thought of him touching her, and no matter how much she showered or took a bath, she couldn't get the smell of him off of her. He left the room that night only to return the next. This time it was one of her sisters he had sex with. Just as he was leaving the room that night, there dad Marcus, caught him coming out of the girl's room and wanted to know what he was doing coming out of the girl's room? Adrienne didn't know what he told their dad, but Marcus came and pulled the covers from the bed, and Adrienne didn't know what made her dad think it was her, but her dad actually thought it was her he was with. She thought, maybe because her gown was the only one up around her waist. Adrienne never got the chance to tell her dad it wasn't her but she got the beating of her life for one of her sisters that next day with what her daddy called a hickory switch and they would be wrapped around each other. Adrienne often got punished for what someone else had done, because she didn't have the courage to stand up for herself for fear of getting hit in the mouth. Whenever she did try to say something, she would get hit in the mouth or anywhere for that matter. Hanna often did that to her. Neither one of her sisters ever came forward or said a word, nor did they apologize to her for having to take their punishment, but Adrienne forgave them in her heart, and they never talked of it again. It was as though it never happened, but Adrienne thought it was worth the beating when her dad threw him out of the house. Adrienne didn't care if she ever saw him again, he was dead to her. He moved to where his sister's were for a while then he went into the army sometime later, and ended up killing himself, at least that was what they told the family, but Adrienne had another theatre, and that is that Billy was made to kill himself. Billy and his girlfriend went into the army at the same time right out of high school. Billy's girlfriend came home with a child, she had with another man while in the army, but Billy married her anyway, and Billy adopted the little girl. Adrienne theatre is that Billy got caught molesting that little girl. His wife brother was on the police force. It was Adrienne's guess that Billy's wife called her brother, and he got to Billy first, making him pull the trigger, that killed him, and then made it look like suicide. Adrienne's sister thinks she got pregnant by Billy, but Adrienne doesn't think so, because Billy had something called yellow jaundice and he would not have been able to have children. So she was told, they never talked about it, it was years later that Adrienne's sister confessed that her oldest son was Billy's child. After Adrienne's sister had her baby she went off to job corp. A training school leaving her baby behind and Adrienne ended up taking care of him while she was away. By the time her sister returned back from job corp. she was pregnant with another child, and Adrienne too was pregnant at sixteen with her first child, she had been date raped by a man that claimed he loved her, but all the time he just wanted her body to satisfy his own selfishness. Adrienne tried to fight him off of her, but he was too strong for her. This man would punch her like he was punching a man, so she gave in to stop him from hitting her. He should have gone to jail for statutory rape. He was almost in his thirties. Once again she didn't tell anyone. It seem that every man she ever came in contact with, well, all but her dad, was only after one thing, and that was sex, she hated sex thinking that it was naught, and degrading having

9

to fight men off of her, and a couple of them were her uncle's. One of her uncle's came over to the house one day, she was in the room using the pot, and he actually tried to pull her up off of the pot. Adrienne had another uncle to try something with her. There was a summer program going on that summer for teenagers that wanted to work, this particular day Adrienne stepmother Hanna didn't have a way to pick her and her cousin up from work, so Hanna asked one of her brother-in laws down the street to pick them up. This was Adrienne's first job away from home. She worked at the head start with little children. Adrienne's uncle passed by her house and took her cousin home first. She thought he was going to take her back home or let her out at his house and she could walk to her house across the street, but instead he went in the opposite direction of where she lived. To a place she had no idea where she was. It was on a dirt road somewhere in the woods. It was some place she had never been before. There was no one else around to help her. Her uncle locked the doors on the car so she couldn't get out, but she fought him off of her, so when he saw that he wasn't getting anywhere, he took her home. She use to would go to his house after he got married, she had gotten close with his wife, but after that incident, she never went there again, Adrienne was fourteen years old at the time. It took her a long time to forgive her uncle. She wanted nothing else to do with him ever again, for him to try something like that with his brother's child was unexceptionable to her. Adrienne was finally able to forgive her uncle and it felt good for her to let her uncle know that she forgave him. She got up the courage one day after she was grown with her own children Once upon a time whenever she would see him, she would speak to him and keep going. You can't trust anyone, not even your own kin. The word tells us to trust no man, but to put your trust in God. Adrienne's first husband, Rick, cared more about sex and alcohol then he did the marriage. Whenever Adrienne wouldn't have sex with Rick, he would get very angry and violent before he forced himself on her, she didn't understand why he was so violent toward her? But sex was far from her mind. Especially after he had put his hands on her. Adrienne didn't know why she didn't just stay away from him, ignorance on her part she guess, although she hadn't been taught about these things, but she used to hear her dad and Hanna fight all the time so she thought it was natural. Because of the hurt and shame she felt, she never told anyone what she was going through, even in high school, she wasn't functioning the way she should have been at all, Her teachers though she needed to be in special education, which she didn't think she did. Adrienne needed glasses but no one bothered to notice. Blaming herself for being with Rick in the first place, Adrienne wanted so desperately to get away from home, that she married her abuser, the man that raped and beat on her whenever he wanted, to get what he wanted, Adrienne thought about how foolish she was. She thought many times of running away from home, but she had no money. Hanna had taken all the money she had worked a whole month for, and only gave Adrienne twenty dollars, and she knew she wasn't going to get very far on that.

All her life Adrienne had been shielded from the world around her, but no one knew the hell she was going through at home. At the age of sixteen the only place she had ever been was school, church and back home, she felt that no one really cared about her, most suddenly not Hanna, she didn't care about Adrienne. Hanna was the one that took Adrienne and Rick to a preacher to get married. She also witnessed the marriage. That's just how much Hanna didn't care. Hanna had never even talked to them about things young girls needed to know about, and to think she was getting rid of Adrienne, her husband and she ended up living in her dad's house until he put them out. Then they went to live with Rick's grandparents and Rick was still so mean to Adrienne. She remembered him throwing the babies bottle into the fireplace, that was the only bottle she had left, Adrienne was trying to get her off the bottle anyway, but slowly. Rick came to the house drunk and wanting to have sex, the baby was crying, Adrienne was trying to fix her bottle; Rick angry as usual took the bottle and threw it in the fireplace. Once again he forced himself on her.

Before Adrienne and Rick were married, Adrienne find out she was pregnant, at the age of sixteen, there was a point in the relationship when Adrienne called it quits with Rick. She got tired of the way he treated her, because she didn't want to have sex with him especially when he was drunk, so he would force himself on her more times then she care to remember. Adrienne met up with a guy by the name of Andrew; they met over the telephone when she dialed his number by accident while trying to call someone else. Andrew liked the sound of her voice and carried on a conversation with her. He was in town visiting with his uncle. Adrienne didn't know anything about him, just his name. They talked all the time on the phone, but had never seen each other in person until one night there was going to be a talent show going on at High school Adrienne attended and they agreed to meet one another there. Adrienne thought Andrew would be different from Rick, since he was the only other man she had talked with other then Rick. Adrienne wanted so much to believe in someone, and that not all men were the same, it still hadn't dawned on her that all he wanted from her was sex. All the men she had come in contact with had one thing on their mind. Adrienne was very nigh eve for her age afraid to say no. Adrienne hadn't been taught anything about sex or told things she needed to know as a young lady. All Adrienne knew was she wanted to be loved not so much as in a sexual way, but for someone to be there for her, to put their arms around her to comfort her to talk to her as she felt so all alone in this great big old world. All she found was hatred and sex craved men at every turn. That was the one and only time she ever laid eyes on Andrew. Adrienne was in a talent show one night along with two other girls. One of them was her cousin and the other one a class maid. After meeting Andrew he wanted Adrienne to walk with him back to his uncle's house that wasn't too from the school where the talent show was going on. Adrienne being ignorant once again thought he wanted her to meet his uncle, but all he wanted too was sex. Adrienne didn't have since enough to say no. After a while Adrienne realized she was pregnant, she didn't know if she became pregnant that night or if she was already pregnant from being raped by Rick. Andrew walked Adrienne back to the school that night and she never saw or heard from him again. Adrienne was looking for love, but in all the wrong places, all she found was men wanting to have sex with her, and to her that's all it was just sex, and she hated it. Somewhere in the back of her mind, it felt wrong because it just didn't feel right, and she didn't know how to stop it without getting beat up. Andrew had left town without even saying goodbye. Adrienne had no idea how to get in touch with him, or if the baby was his, or was it Rick's. It was years later that Adrienne decided to look up Andrew's Uncle Bob to see if he knew where Andrew was, and to her surprise Adrienne learned that Andrew was a married man at the time he was visiting with his Uncle, and had one or two children. He and his wife were separated. Adrienne learned too that Andrew had passed away sometime after he went back home.

Adrienne met Rick, when one day she followed her sister to meet with her boyfriend. Adrienne was to meet her sister's boyfriend brother which turned out to be Rick. Instead of them going to school where they were supposed to be. That was the first time Adrienne had ever sipped school. She liked the attention Rick was giving her at first, he would buy her things, but she was afraid to take them home with her because she would not have been able to explain where they came from. Then things got very ugly when she didn't want to have sex with Rick, he would hit her forcing himself on her. Adrienne thought it was going to be just that one time thing but then she realized every time she saw him all he wanted was sex. Rick started out being so nice and buying her things, then it dawned on Adrienne that he wanted something in return. Adrienne was looking for the love she wasn't getting at home. She missed her mother's love and her daddy's love as well even though they lived in the same house, but there was no love in the house at all, the house she had to call home it was everything but a home. The constant hollowing, fighting, the cursing, and hitting made her very nerve and angry all at the same time, it was just not in her to treat people the way they treated her. Adrienne was suffering in silence and thought maybe that was why she was always picked on all the time. She was the quiet type that stayed to herself in the room where she slept listening to music away from everybody else wishing she was any where else but there, but trouble found her no matter where she was. She'd get the blame for what someone else did. The man that her dad was was the type of men she came in contact with some way or another. Angry, loud, arrogant and abusive men and Rick was an angry, all the time drinking, and abusive man. Adrienne was slow to comprehend things sometime, this was something she always tried hard to hide for fear of saying something wrong, sometime saying nothing at all, but she would be only telling the truth, and telling the truth got her in a lot of trouble. To stay out of trouble Adrienne kept busy trying to help and care for others to hide the pain of what she was going through that she forgot to take care of herself. Adrienne sacrificed a lot of herself by having compassion for others, although it was never appreciated. Adrienne was taught how to work by her dad, Hanna and her grandmother so much that that was pretty much all she knew how to do was work. She had heard of God and His Son Jesus Christ, but trying to cope on her own with what she was going through, left her not understanding who they were. The devil had her life sit up to fail by keeping her so wrapped up in her problems that she couldn't hear what God was saying to her even though she had ears to hear, and her eyes from seeing even though she had eyes. Adrienne was embarrassed to say, but she didn't know God was there to help her, and that God gave His Son Jesus to die for her sins, and the rest of the world. If only she had known to ask the Savior to help her at a young age. The message was in the song, but she just didn't get it at the time. Adrienne believed her life would have been different, if it hadn't taken her so long to catch on to things, and then again only God knows. Adrienne remembered the message was in the song they sung at church, "Ask the Savior to help you." but she didn't get it at the time they were singing it, she thought it was just a song. It hadn't dawned on her that there was message in every song. Adrienne's dad Marcus was always away from home working. It was dark outside when he left home going to work, and when he came back. All the children had to be in bed at eight o'clock on the dot each night, no matter what. Adrienne tried very hard to do what she was told. She didn't like getting whipped but nothing she did was ever good enough, no matter how hard she tried.

While Marcus was busy working he never knew Hanna was cheating on him with one of his friends. Adrienne knew, but she didn't want to be the one to hurt her dad that way. She never told her dad or anyone, but it was during the time Adrienne was pregnant with her first child. Once again she was the only one at home with Hanna. Adrienne had to quit school after finding out she was pregnant. Hanna would dress up, put on her makeup, comb her hair and tell Adrienne she was going to the store, and she would leave the house walking as if she was walking to the store a mile or so up the street from the house. One day Adrienne decided to look out the window and this orange truck came by and picked Hanna up, she was gone for hours leaving Adrienne to do the cooking and cleaning. Hanna returned home just before the school bus dropped the other children off at home. Adrienne was often blamed for what someone else had done; she didn't understand why it was so hard for her to stand up for herself. Most of the time she didn't know what was going on around her, and she never had very much to say keeping beauty much to herself.

She would get a beating and most of the time she didn't know why? It was always Adrienne did it, and she would think to herself, did what? There wasn't a day that went by she didn't get blamed for something it seemed. Adrienne had a stepsister that accused her of breaking her glasses, and Adrienne had no idea what had happened to her glasses, but got the whipping for them being broken. Adrienne tried to stay away from trouble, but trouble found her. She didn't understand much about good and evil, but she was experiencing evil on a daily bases. Nothing good it seemed ever happened to her, no matter wish way she turned. She didn't know it was the devil trying to kill her, and used those people that were the closest to her, but she tried hard to teach her own children the best she knew how. While at the same time she was trying not to be the evil person Hanna was to her and others around her. Adrienne didn't know to teach her children about God and Jesus, but she carried or sent them to church the way her dad did her, but he didn't go to church unless it was a funeral or revival. Adrienne tried to do good by helping others, but the more she did the more she was envied and hated by those around her. Adrienne continued to treat others the way she wanted to be treated, being very much disappointed when she didn't get that same good treatment in return.

At sixteen, Adrienne thought after having her baby, she would have that love she so desperately wanted and needed in her life. Adrienne was ignorant to the word of God, even though she went to church and sometime read the bible. Adrienne didn't realize she was being disobedient to the word of God by having sex and bring a child into the world, and she wasn't married, while still being a child herself. It wasn't her intention to have sex or a child, but under the circumstances, she thanked God for her child and asked God for forgiveness. At seventeen, life for Adrienne was devastating, even more after she married the man she thought to be her baby's dad thinking it was the right thing to do. Oh how wrong was she, things went from bad to worse. Nothing about Rick changed, he was very abusive still, and drank too much for Adrienne. He cheated on her, and stayed away from home days at a time. Adrienne was young, but she knew that wasn't right for him to not come home. Rick didn't know how to be a husband, and Adrienne was too young to know that sex was a part of being a wife. In the back of Adrienne's mind, she thought sex was dirt and nasty because she had been violated she really didn't like being touched. She just needed someone to hold her like a mother would and tell her everything was going to be all right. She married Rick thinking she could change him into being a good husband instead of waiting on God to send her the husband He had for her. What a big mistake that was, all Rick thought about was sex, and Adrienne was by no means ready for that at all, she guess he thought he could beat her into having sex with him, which he did most of the time force himself on her. If Rick hadn't been drunk all the time, he would have realized she was unlearned when it came to sex and instead of him being patient with her, and loving her like a husband is suppose to love his wife, he thought he would use his fist. Adrienne may not have known much about what it meant to be married, and she was taught nothing at all about sex, it was forced on her. Every time Rick put his hands on her made her dislike him even more, well not so much him, but his ways. Adrienne realized she may have been wrong to withhold sex from him, but she didn't know she would have to have sex with him any time he wanted. Adrienne didn't know where he had been or whom he was with for three or four days at a time. When he did decide to come home, he would be angry. Adrienne wished he had stayed where he was. Rick would come in the house drunk and angry, hitting her as though she was a man, busting open her forehead with his fist because she didn't want him touching her especially when he had been drinking, and gone for three and four days at a time. Adrienne didn't know where Rick was, whom he was with, if dead or alive until he came staggering through the door drunk, and ready to fight if he couldn't have his way with her. Adrienne couldn't stand the thought of Rick touching her rather he was drunk or sober after being so mean and abusive toward her, although he was that way before they got married. She couldn't understand what made her think he would be any different after they were married, but she married him to get away from abuse at home and ran head on into more abuse from Rick. It was the wrong thing for Adrienne to do, and foolish on her part, but the more abuse she got from Rick let her know he didn't care anything about her at all. Adrienne thought he could have at least explained to her about sex, and had some compassion instead of anger toward her; all she wanted was some peace and happiness. Just when she thought things couldn't get any worse, they did. She had to go to work a lot of days with a black eye, bruises, and scratches where Rick had jumped on her. She tried her best to hide it with makeup so no one could see it and ask her questions. She didn't want to explain about where they had come from, and people just wouldn't mine their own business. People were already talking about her behind her back. People she didn't even know had a lot to say about her and they didn't know her at all. She didn't have any one she could call her friend. Having to go out into the world and find a job, people can look at you and not like you for whatever reason. They didn't have to know, just wanted to be all up in other people business so they'd have something to talk about behind your back, and then again, Adrienne thought maybe she should have told someone. She wondered how could she of keep silence with what she was dealing with on her own? Hanna had told Adrienne that whatever went on in the house stayed in the house. After what Adrienne had gone through as a child, it was always in the back of her mind that she had her innocents taken away from her before she was ready, and she could never get that back. She would never get the chance to experience the pleasure of making love for the first time with the man that God intended to be her husband and life partner for the rest of her life. On top of that Adrienne found out later on that Rick was already married to another woman. Rick was off somewhere as usual and a woman called for him at his grandparent house and Adrienne answered the phone. The woman asked for Rick, but he wasn't there, she then wanted to know who Adrienne was, and she told the woman she was Rick wife, and the woman asked Adrienne how could she be Rick's wife when she was his wife? That let Adrienne know that Rick and the woman hadn't gotten a divorce. That was good for Adrienne to know because it made it just that much easier for her to walk away after a year of being in hell with him. Adrienne woke up after Rick hit her twice in the head with a wine bottle. Adrienne knew after that she had had enough of him his being drunk and his beating on her. She decided she could do badly all by herself and she wasn't going to take his abusiveness anymore. Adrienne learned to drive running from Rick, after one driving lesson from her brother. She made it to the car and got away before Rick could pull the plugs out of the car the way he sometime did. Adrienne went back to her dad's house. Rick went looking for her, but she had made up in her mind she was not about to go back with him, it was over. Rick grabbed Audrey and put her in the car while she was outside playing in the yard, taking her with him when he realized Adrienne was serious about not going back with him. Rick thought about it when he got down the road, and turned around bring Audrey back to her mother. Rick must have known Adrienne was going to call the police on him the reason he decided to bring her back. Rick was never a father to Audrey; he stayed too drunk to even be a husband. After Adrienne left Rick it wasn't long before Adrienne found a small house for rent for her and her daughter to live in. She didn't look back, after Hanna told her she had to move out. It had something Hanna said, to do with her getting food stamps, but Adrienne knew it was a lie for Hanna to get reed of her the way she always tried to do, and that was fine with Adrienne because she didn't want to live their anyway. Adrienne sometime later heard that Rick had moved to Chicago. She hadn't seen or heard from him for years, and all of a sudden, one day he calls Adrienne's dad house looking for her. Rick left a number for her to call him; he was somehow avoiding paying her child support which he hasn't paid even this day. With the help of the Lord, Adrienne had to raise Audrey on her own. Rick would always tell Adrienne he was going to send Audrey something, but she never got it, all Rick ever sent her was fifty dollars the whole time she was growing up. Audrey was a teenager age fifteen when she wanted to know who her dad was. Adrienne let Audrey decide if she wanted a relationship with her dad or not, so when Audrey tried to get to know Rick, he didn't have time to be there for her. Rick was always telling her he was going to do this and that, but he never came through for her, and she got tied of him lying to her and she decided for a long time that she didn't have a dad. He just didn't seem to care that he was hurting her not being there for her. He was a disappointment to her, but Adrienne thank God, He was a Father for her baby girl down through the years. She grew up to be a good, beautiful and talented young lady inside and out. Adrienne prayed God's Blessings upon all her children, her grandchildren, and their children the way her grandmother did for her.

CHAPTER TWO

Having a daughter of her own Adrienne tried very hard to keep her safe from the abuse that she herself had endured as a child, a teenager, and then an adult. She tried to teach her child the way she knew her mother would have taught her had she lived to raise her children herself. Adrienne's dad told her, that her mother died of an enlarged heart. After years of being told her mother died of pneumonia by other people who knew her. While wanting to know more about her mother, what she was like and how she died. When visiting with her uncle, her mother's brother one summer in New York at the age of fifteen Adrienne turned sixteen while she was were. Adrienne read pages of a letter her mother had written about her life when she was married to her dad, and they were not happy times for her mother, but everything within Adrienne told her that her mother died of a broken heart. As her dad so often cheated on her mother over and over again. He even cheated on her with the woman Adrienne had to call her stepmother. Adrienne's dad left her mother with three children to be with the woman he cheated on her mother with. Adrienne could feel her mother's hurt in her, as she too had been cheated on time after time. Adrienne could feel that her mother had a kind heart. Her mother was loving, caring, forgiving, and a giving person to others, so much that she too forgot to take care of herself. Adrienne realized she was just like her mother, putting everyone else needs and feelings before her own. Wanting to save the world, but couldn't, not knowing how to say no to anyone, only to get their hearts broken in the end. All Adrienne had of her mother's was a picture and very few memories of her. People that knew her mother said, she was a very nice person, and that she too liked doing hair, as did Adrienne. Adrienne being just like her mother knew she would laugh to keep from crying. She cried when she had had enough of being treated wrong. No one knew the sadness and pain she had on the inside. Adrienne tried so desperately to hide the sadness and pain, but was beginning to realize

God was, and still is by her side. It was the ways of man Adrienne hated the most, feeling the pain of her mother so much that their were times that she herself wanted to give up and die just to be with her mother. Adrienne got to the point where she just wanted to fall asleep never to awake to this world again. Adrienne somehow knew her mother loved her dad so much that each time she took him back only for him to cheat on her again with someone else. He just wasn't strong enough to love her back. Even after all her mother went through with him he walked off and left her with three children for a woman he knew nothing about. Hanna had four children of her own. Marcus, Adrienne's dad left his children with Hanna not knowing she was going to abuse his children the minute his back was turned. Hanna had no idea she was going to have to rise Marcus's children after his first wife died. Hanna ended up cheating on Marcus the same way he cheated on Adrienne's mother. Adrienne knew that God would be the judge of that. It was Hanna's fought that Adrienne brother went to prison. He got caught stealing something for Hanna. Hanna went as far as to call Adrienne uncle in New York to tell him her dad was having sex with her sister his own daughter, which was a lie. Hanna knew it was her son molesting both Adrienne and her sister. That was how they ended up going to New York that summer. Hanna wasn't looking for them to ever come back home. After Adrienne dad agreed to let them go. Hanna did whatever she could to get reed of Marcus three children anyway she could. Marcus didn't have a clue what was going on. Adrienne's Uncle Ted was under the impression Adrienne and her sister were there to stay. Auntie, they called their Uncle's wife, had registered them in school there already but Adrienne dad said, for their Uncle to send them home. Adrienne really wished she could have stayed rather then go back to the abuse. It was getting close to time for school to start back home. Adrienne's dad called their Uncle wanting to know why they hadn't come home yet. Adrienne's Uncle Ted did send them back on the bus. Adrienne could tell her Uncle was hurt having to send them back after Hanna lied to him, and Adrienne was too that they had to go back home. Adrienne liked it there with her Uncle on her mother's side of the family, her Auntie and cousins whom they had never met before. It took three days for Adrienne and her sister to get back home. Their Uncle gave them five dollars a piece for food but he didn't tell them it was going to be three days before they got home. It cost to use the bathroom whenever the bus stopped at the bus stop for a lay over. It was Adrienne's Uncle that recognized the fact that she needed glasses, and brought her, her first pair of glasses. Adrienne had gone most of her school years needing glasses, and her Uncle was the only one to take the time to notice. Adrienne remember her grandmother on her mother's side, sending her and her sister boxes of clothes all the way from California, and they never got to wear any of them, because Hanna took them and wore them herself. Hanna was so mean to Adrienne. It was like the story Cinderella and the wick stepmother. Hanna treated her own children better then she treated Adrienne, her sister and brother. So did her dad. He did whatever Hanna told him.

Once Adrienne and her sister returned home they found out her sister was pregnant. It was years later when Adrienne realized the same guy that tried to rape her was the father of her sister's baby.

Adrienne didn't know if this guy had raped her or what? Adrienne never asked her any questions about it. Adrienne had to fight this same guy off of her. She never told her sister that that was the same guy who pretended he wanted to show her something in the house and when they were inside the house, he locked the door behind them so she couldn't get out, but Adrienne fought him off of her until he got tied. Once Adrienne found a chance to get to the door, she took it and ran not stopping until she was at her Uncle's house. Adrienne fought him hard trying to keep him off of her he was strong, but Adrienne made it to the door and unlocked it before he could get her pants off. She didn't know how to say no, but she had made up in her mind the only way he was going to get that was take it and she was not going to make it easy for him. Once again Adrienne didn't tell any one about it including her sister.

At the age of seventeen, Adrienne moved out on her own, and it wasn't her choice. It was very scary for her at first so much she couldn't sleep at night, even though she wasn't alone, her daughter Audrey was there with her, but she was just a baby. Adrienne knew it was her job to protect her child. She would be lying in bed at night trying her best to fall asleep, but the sleep wouldn't come until it was almost time for her to get up for work, but by that time she was so exhausted she couldn't get out of bed sometime. The fear of having to leave her child with Hanna the woman that was so mean and abusive to her as a child made her have a very uneasy feeling about this woman keeping her child.

She was at the point of exhaustion trying to work and worried about everything not knowing what else to do or who else she could get that would keep her child. At seventeen Adrienne didn't know anyone else. Her daddy was so strict on them that she didn't get to socialize with other people much unless they were family members, and she only got to see them every once in a while. Only God knows what was happening to her child while she was at work. The same way only God knows what was happening to her while her daddy was at work. There were day's Adrienne was so tried that she couldn't get up to go to work for lack of sleep. Several times she almost lost her job because she hadn't had much sleep, but she knew she had to take care of her child on her own. She didn't have any help from Audrey's daddy from day one. Adrienne continued to go to church even though she didn't understand much of what was being said she realized that had she understood more about God and Jesus and prayed to Him personally for help things would have been a lot different in her life. Who knows, maybe it was Gods plan for her life, so that she would learn to have faith and trust in Him. It was from the like of understanding and ignorance on her part, which made it hard for her to cope with life's trails and tribulations. Five years went by as Adrienne struggled on her own to make a life for her and her child praying that God would send her a husband. When she should have been praying for God to take care of her and her child. Adrienne met husband two thinking that God had sent him.

Walker, was dating a friend of Adrienne's at the time, and as she started to remember. She had decided to stop hanging out at the clubs, where she would be every Friday, Saturday and sometime Sunday nights at a hot spot where she liked to hang out miles from where she lived. Sometime she would go to a club in Mason but the first time she went out to a club was with Rick. She remembered they had gone out to a club in the city. The world was so different then what she was use to, so much so that she felt out of place. Rick and she were on the dance floor and when the music stopped, and they were on there way back to the table, when all of a sudden, some guy grabbed her by the arm pulling her back onto the dance floor. Wanting her to dance with him. She had never been out to a club before, the music was right so she danced with the guy. Adrienne didn't know what to expect, but when she got back to the table where Rick was, he let her have it with a slap right across the face. Adrienne being the kind of person she was; was so embarrassed to make a seen that she didn't do or say anything. But when she got home, that's was when she called off the relationship with him. She then started going to the club with her cousins, and her sister. She liked dancing, Adrienne started going to the club at the age of seventeen, and by the time she was twenty-one, she realized the clubs was not a place for her to be. At the same time she was going to church on Sunday morning. She ran into some of the other church members there as well. There was too much fighting, stabbing, and shooting going on for her at the club, so she decided it would be best for her if she just stopped going out to the club. She started hanging out at this woman house on Friday and Saturday night. She met Annie Mae through Annie Mae's brother Jim. Adrienne and Jim would get together whenever he came to town. Annie Mae would have a card game going on where they played cards for money, their was some whiskey and beer drinking going on too, but Adrienne wasn't a drinker and didn't want to start after putting up with Rick drunk self all the time. Adrienne couldn't play cards well enough to play so she was in charge of cooking and selling fish sandwiches. A guy by the name of Walker came into the kitchen to buy a fish sandwich, he was checking out the help, which was Adrienne. She didn't know it at the time, but it was the next day after staying the night at Annie Mae's house that Friday night. Annie Mae invited Adrienne to go with her and her daughter to a wedding that Saturday at Church Of God and Christ and that was when Walker made his move. He told Adrienne that he was interested in her. Adrienne knew Walker was with her friend Gale the night before. Walker denied there was anything between the two of them. Walker had a friend with him that Friday night that tried all night long to have sex with Adrienne, but she wasn't interested in him. Walker lied to Adrienne when he told her he wasn't with her friend Annie Mae's daughter that night, but they had just met that same night. Walker shared with Adrienne that he was new in town, and that her friend and him had just met through his friend. Walker friend wanted to be with Adrienne, but Adrienne didn't want to be with him. Come to find out, Walker friend Clayton was in town to visit another woman he was dating. Walker made his move on Adrienne at the wedding telling her he wanted to be with her, and like a fool she fall for his lie. After the wedding Walker left the church with Adrienne. It wasn't until later on that night that she realized she had hurt her friend Gale when she stopped by her house to pickup the beautiful dress that she had let Adrienne borrow for the wedding. It hurt Adrienne to know that she had hurt her friend. Adrienne didn't know what to say to Gale, but from the way Gale was talking there was something going on between her and Walker. Walker just sat there as if he hadn't done anything saying nothing, Adrienne thought if Walker didn't want to be with her friend Gale, he should have told her instead of leading her on. Walker stayed with Adrienne that night. A few days later something was going on with Walker. He got up one morning asking Adrienne if he could use her car. He said to Adrienne he was going over to the apartment where he was living to get some of his things. When he returned he blamed Adrienne for giving him a sexually transmitted disease. Adrienne wasn't dating anyone before Walker. That let Adrienne know Walker was with her friend the night before the two of them got together. Adrienne wasn't sure who gave it to whom, but she suspect Walker gave it to her since he was with her friend's daughter the night before. Adrienne felt as though she was in to deep to turn back now. She had feelings for Walker and didn't have the courage to break it off. She wanted to help Walker get back on his feet since he had become homeless with no place to stay, no food, no money, and no job. Maybe that should have told her something, but she though she would want someone to help her if she were in his shoes. Adrienne was a care giver, she always looked for the good in people, and from the goodness of her heart she was willing to give him a chance to get on his feet since he had no close family around to help him. Adrienne told Walker after thinking they could help each other. He needed a place to stay and she needed a man around to help her around the house. The guy Walker was sharing an apartment with Clayton left Walker there in the apartment and went back to California. Clayton was mad with Walker because Adrienne chose Walker over him. Walker claim he didn't know when Clayton was coming back or if he was coming back. Adrienne went by the apartment to see Walker, he was laying on the couch in a strange place. He had no food in the apartment or money to buy food with, and he didn't know anyone. Adrienne being the caring person she was felt sorry for him not having any money or food. Adrienne had her bill money in her purse, she took it and brought Walker some food to hold him for a few days in hope that he would find a job. Adrienne lived along with her daughter, but at the end of the month Walker had to move out of the apartment and he had no money for the next month rent. Adrienne could barely pay her own rent. She let Walker move in with her. He didn't even have a way of getting around, all he had was a suitcase with a few clothes in it. Adrienne let him use her car to get around to look for a job. While at the same time she was putting in a word for him on her job to one of the supervisors at the factory. Walker had her fooled for a while, Adrienne thought he was the best thing to happen to her. Walker being all nice at first, cooking and cleaning while she went to work. Sometime they would go on a long drive looking at the country side view, but what Adrienne didn't know was that Walker was learning his way around town, which was good in a way. They sometime went to the lake for a picnic, or to the movies, just having fun together. Walker would sometime barrow Adrienne's car to go off by himself. It turned out Walker knew more about how to get around in her hometown then she did. Enjoying each other company they took long bathes together. They went out to dinner, to the park, they went to the fair when it was in town, to the grocery store, shopping, they did everything together, they worked in the yard together, they even went to church together, when you saw one you saw the other. Adrienne even brought herself another car, giving Walker the car she had so he would have a way of getting around without having to barrow Adrienne's car. Adrienne thought she was doing something good to help him and she wouldn't be stranded at home when he was gone in her car and she needed to go somewhere. It had gotten to the point where Walker would be gone for hours at a time. Walker would tell Adrienne he was going to the store for a newspaper but he always came back drunk. One morning Walker stayed out all night drinking and gambling, until four o'clock in the morning, so he said. Adrienne was upset that he was out all night, but she was such an easy going person she forgave him for whatever he did. Like the Lord said for us to do in His word. But look like the more she forgave him the worse he became. Still she looked for the good in people even before she knew who God was and still is. Adrienne made the mistake of telling Walker about her first husband, how he treated her, with his drinking, beating on her, and staying away from home days at a time. It wasn't long that Walker began to treat her the same way her first husband Rick did. Slowly things began to change for the worse with Walker. No matter how hard Adrienne tried to make things better between them. Hoping things would go back to the way they were at first. The harder Walker fought against her, letting the devil use him while controlling every minute of her day with his jealousy and rage. Hitting her, using her as his punching bag every time things didn't go his way. Calling her out of her name, names that cut like a knife, keeping her from her family. During the holidays, Thanksgiving and Christmas they ended up at his family's. Adrienne was so exhausted. There were times when she just wanted to stay at home and rest, but Walker wanted to see his mother, stepfather, and sister.

The drive was six to seven hours long. Adrienne had to help with the driving. It got to where Adrienne couldn't have any friends. She didn't mine so much about that. She didn't have time for any friends anyway. There was always something to do at home when she got off work. But Walker made sure she didn't have any friends at all. Now he could go off and talk to anybody he wanted, while watching Adrienne every move.

Audrey was Adrienne's baby girl. She wasn't much trouble at all. She was a very smart little girl. Adrienne wanted to be for her the mother that she didn't have growing up. Adrienne always brought educational toys for Audrey, something she could learn from. Adrienne would read to her, and before she knew it, Audrey was reading to her. Adrienne brought her a big toy box that she could write her ABC's on. The toy box had the alphabets written on it, and Audrey would write them all by herself. Audrey was writing and spelling her own name before she went off to head start. Adrienne second child Ariel was a daddy's girl. Walker turned their child Ariel against her mother by letting Ariel have her way. Walker would let Ariel have her way with whatever she wanted to do. Most of the time it was something she didn't have any business doing. Walker did things and let Ariel do things just to hurt Adrienne. But little did Walker know, he was hurting Ariel too, health wise. If Adrienne said to Ariel eat your vegetables. Walker would tell her she didn't have to eat them. All Ariel wanted was something sweet to eat. Walker would tell her to go a head and eat her dessert.

Once Walker got up on his feet with a job, a car, and everything he needed. He didn't need Adrienne anymore. Walker thought that getting drunk was going to solve his problems. When he drank he was a totally different person. On Friday night he had to go off drinking with his friends while Adrienne was at home taking care of the children. Doing the cooking and cleaning being that virtuous woman, even though they were not yet married. Out of jealousy, Walker friends would say something to him concerning Adrienne and he believed whatever they said. They didn't like the fact that he came in from out of town and got the woman they had been trying to get for themselves. Walker would come in drunk, mad and ready to fight. He knew Adrienne wasn't going to fight him back. She could have, but that would have made her no better then him. The next morning Walker would apologize, then promise never to hit her again. But he did time after time. Then he would tell her why he jumped on her in the beginning. Adrienne knew what his friends were doing, but Walker was to drunk to see that they were not his friends. It would be about something Adrienne had no idea what he was talking about. Walker friends wanted him to think they knew Adrienne, and like a fool he fail for their lies.

When Adrienne became pregnant with Ariel after having several miscarriages made Walker happy for a minute, but it didn't stop him from going out drinking with his friends whenever he wanted. Adrienne could tell whenever he'd been drinking. She could smell him coming. Adrienne had a difficult pregnancy so was her first. She was sick all the time, any and everything made her sick including Walker. After Ariel was born, Walker didn't want anyone to breathe on her hard. Adrienne had to take Ariel and herself to the doctor for their checkup. Adrienne decided to stop by her job to let everyone see her baby. Which all the ladies did that had babies, Walker got so angry with Adrienne wanting to know why she brought his daughter around all those germs as if she was to good for people to see or something, Ariel was his heart, Walker couldn't say no to her. Adrienne thought, maybe he acted that way because Ariel was his only daughter. Walker went out in search of a bigger house after Ariel was born. The house they lived in was kind of small for four people. But it was just across the street almost from the church they attended. They moved to town, which was close to walking distant of town. While attending church often, Adrienne realized after three years of them living together. They were living together in sin by not being married. Adrienne was trying to change her way of living so she talked Walker into them getting married, hoping that it would make things better in both their lives. But things just went from bad to worse after the wedding.

Walker and Adrienne both had been married before. Walker had two grown sons. One of his sons his wife had with someone else before they were married. For some reason every time Walker got mad with Adrienne, he would get on the phone and call his ex-wife. It was as though they had some unfinished issues, which made her think what had she gotten herself into this time. That was when Walker told Adrienne he had a twenty-one year old son who had been in prison. Adrienne didn't think much about it until he came back telling her he wanted his son to come and visit with them for two weeks. Adrienne thought, she would finally get to see the face that went alone with the name Walker Jr. It wasn't long after Walker Junior arrived that Walker started acting nice compared to the way he usually acted toward her. He came back to tell her his son was going to stay with them for a while because he had gotten into some trouble and he didn't want him going back to prison. It had something to do with drugs. Adrienne's mind quickly flashed back to what had happened to her in her childhood. She didn't want that same thing happening to her girls, so she told Walker she didn't think it was search a good idea, but before she could explain to him why? He got mad and didn't want to hear what she had to say. If Walker could have talked to Adrienne before he made the decision on his own, there would have had a better out come. But Walker wanted to make the decisions and then talk to Adrienne about them. He treated Adrienne very cold after he couldn't have his way, by not talking to her for days at a time. Except for when other people were around. In public Walker pretended everything was good between him and Adrienne, putting on an act for man. Walker went on to make it his life's mission to destroy Adrienne after putting his son on a bus back to California when the two weeks were up. It was Walker plan all alone for Walker Junior to stay with them without talking to Adrienne about it first. But thought he would get Walker Junior to Mississippi first, then tell Adrienne what he was planning to do. All the things they use to do together they no longer did them anymore, including going to church together in the same car. Walker decided he would drive his car and Adrienne would drive her car, and they were both going to the same place. Walker put on a show at church when he went to the pastor behind Adrienne's back. He didn't tell the pastor the truth about what was going on. But told the pastor what he wanted him to know. Making Adrienne out to be the bad person, while making his self look good as usual. The pastor called Adrienne into his office after she got to church wanting to talk to her. Adrienne told the pastor truth about what was going on the best she could. Adrienne could have told the pastor Walker was an abusive husband, but she didn't out of shame. And she didn't want their business out there like that. Walker was fourteen years older then she was. Like a fool she was to young to be with him in the first place. But for some reason Adrienne liked older men, but not that much older. She didn't know why she had this thing for older men, but she did. Then Adrienne thought she was more like her grandmother then she knew. Her grandfather was older then her grandmother when they married. Adrienne got up one Sunday morning, this was before the Lord blessed her with another car, she got up to get the girls and herself ready for Sunday school and worship service, as she was combing one of the girls hair. Walker decided he was going to get a newspaper, at lest that was what he told Adrienne he was going to do. Nine thirty comes, no Walker. Sunday school starts at nine thirty, eleven o'clock comes, and still no Walker. Three o'clock still no Walker. Church was long over. Adrienne was so angry with Walker that she took the girls and started walking to where she thought Walker might be. Which was a place he hung out drinking with the boys, and only God knows what else he was doing. By the time they got to the places were she thought Walker was, he wasn't there. Adrienne and the girls walked back home just in time to find Walker and a bunch of guys sitting in their living room drunk. You could smell that they had been drinking. Adrienne was so angry because Walker knew they were going to church before he decided to go in a different direction. All of them smelling like they had been inside the whiskey barrel instead of drinking it. Adrienne asked all of them to leave the house telling Walker he could go with them if he wanted too. Walker jumped up, pushing Adrienne backward telling her he wasn't going anywhere. Before Adrienne knew what was happening, she had picked up an end table and popped Walker across the head with it. To push her was the one thing that made her lose control. Out of all the times he had beat her for no reason, she never defended herself. But when he pushed her it was on. He had gone too far. Adrienne couldn't believe she had done that, but she had had enough of him and his ways. Adrienne thought to her self, you hit me all you want too, but don't ever push me. Adrienne's oldest daughter Audrey went next door and called the police. When they got their Walker was nowhere to be found. But later on that night after the police were gone Walker came crawling from under the house with blood running down his face from where Adrienne had popped him across the head with the end table. Later that night as Adrienne was ironing her clothes for work the next day, Walker thought he would try Adrienne again so he started up an argument with her. Walker was mad still because Adrienne had never hit him before and blood was coming out too. Adrienne had made up in her mind that night that he was never going to hit her again and get away with it. He wanted to get Adrienne back so he rushed toward her to attack her again. But to his surprise, she was ready for him. She held up the hot iron in her hand telling him to come on. She dared him to ever hit her again. She was going to stick that hot iron to him, and show him just how crazy she was, since he was going around telling people she was crazy. If not wanting Walker beating on her meant she was crazy, then so be it. Adrienne had had enough of being his punching bag. For years he abused her in front of their children. It didn't make any difference to Walker he would say anything to her, and about her, but he never hit her again after that day. But he went full force with the verbal abuse. Walker though if he couldn't get her one way, he would get her another. He traded in the car Adrienne had given him for a truck. He put in dark tinted windows so dark you couldn't see inside of it. Walker own mother told Adrienne he was a mean evil man. She should know after being married to his father for some time. And Walker being her son, the fruit didn't fall to far from the tree. Walker mother told Adrienne she shouldn't have anymore children with Walker. Adrienne didn't know what his mother meant by that at the time, but Adrienne found out she was pregnant with their second child already while they were on vacation at his mom house. Adrienne could see that Walker had spoiled Ariel already. Walker didn't want anyone not even Adrienne, or his mother to discipline Ariel. For the things she did wrong. Ariel would take a whole jar of Vaseline and grease herself down with it from head to toe. Or she would pour out the rubbing alcohol and fill the bottle with water. Or she would just mix up stuff like Adrienne's perfumes, whatever she could get her hands on. Walker thought everything Ariel did wrong was funny, because Adrienne was the one that had to clean up after her. Walker even taught Ariel to call Adrienne old meany instead of mama. Whatever Adrienne told Ariel to do. Walker would tell her to do the opposite. He contradicted Adrienne's ever word right in front of Ariel and she caught on to that and used it to her advantage. Walker let her have her way just to get back at Adrienne. Things got so bad that Ariel wouldn't do anything Adrienne asked her to do. Ariel kept a wedge between Walker and Adrienne all the time. Adrienne had several miscarriages before and after the birth of Ariel. At the time Adrienne didn't know it was due to stress from Walker violent behavior, and verbal abuse toward her, and stress on her job. Before Ariel was born, Adrienne was taking some vitamins, because she was tied all the time. She had no energy left in her after working all day. Adrienne managed to get pregnant and carried Ariel for nine months. She managed to get pregnant again but this time she had an abortion. As stressed as she was she probably would have lost it. Adrienne was very sick all the time and she didn't want to be sick anymore.

She just wanted what she was feeling to go away not thinking if it was the right or wrong thing to do. But Adrienne regrets having an abortion afterwards. Adrienne didn't know at the time that what she was feeling was stress, depression, and anxiety. Adrienne repented later on asking God for forgiveness after realizing she had sinned. All those years of going to church, she should have known having an abortion was wrong. The devil had Adrienne's mind so focused on her problems instead what the Lord was saying to her, that she couldn't hear the Lord talking to her. Ariel was in kindergarten. Walker took her to kindergarten class every day. Adrienne worked during the day, and Walker worked at night, so he had time to take her to school after Adrienne had gone to work. The school was just across the street. For some reason he didn't like to hear Ariel cry. She realized that as a baby that her daddy didn't like for her to cry, and she used that as a way of getting whatever she wanted. She had Walker wrapped around her little finger. What she wanted most was all was food and Walker gave it to her rather she was hungry or not just so he wouldn't have to hear her cry. Walker couldn't see that giving her food to keep her quiet was causing her to be extremely overweight as she got older. Adrienne couldn't understand why every time she brought clothes for Ariel she was wearing a bigger size? She went as far as to take Ariel to a specialist and couldn't find anything wrong with her. The doctor wouldn't say right out and tell Adrienne she was eating too much but made it seem as though the weight wasn't bothering her at her age. The doctor gave Adrienne a diet plan to put her on a diet. The diet was working until Adrienne finally realized why Ariel was over weight. Walker had gotten to were every time he wanted to get in the streets Ariel would want to go with him so he would pick a fight with Adrienne. He would take Ariel to the store and buy her a bag of candy, bring her back to the house, sit her down in the middle of the floor, and let her eat the whole bag. He dared Adrienne to say anything to her or try to take it away from her. Then he would leave again this time without her. He had to get to that other woman. He used a public phone on the corner of town to call her when he had a phone at home. Adrienne received a phone call late one Sunday even after church and she was asked why her husband was always on the phone on the corner? Evidently he was seen their more then once or twice. Adrienne knew he wasn't talking to her. Walker must have forgot he was in a small town. When Adrienne confronted him about it, he claimed to be calling his son. But Adrienne knew that was a lie, all of a sudden he had to leave the house to call his son? Doing Ariel first and second grade year in school she was on the Honor roll. She was so happy to be going to big school and riding the bus with her big sister. When she got in the third grade Adrienne heard Walker tell Ariel that she didn't have to do any thing she didn't want to do. Her grades started to go down hill from there. Ariel had to repeat the third grade because of him. Adrienne felt she had no control what so ever over her own child because of him controlling and contradicting every word Adrienne said to her right in front of Ariel. Adrienne never had much trouble with Audrey. She was quiet like Adrienne, and smart. Adrienne thinks Walker was jealous of the fact that Audrey was so smart. Audrey saw in Walker what Adrienne couldn't see, or didn't want to see until it was to late. Adrienne remember coming home from work one day. She had a tiny board that she had written Audrey name on.

It was just the two of them at the time. It was to let Audrey know she would wipe her if she did something wrong. When Adrienne got home from work the board was broken. She asked Walker what happened to the board. He told her he had wiped Audrey with it and it broke. Adrienne thought Walker had to hit her very hard with that board for it to break. She asked him never to hit her again that was her job. Walker hit her again after that but Adrienne didn't know about it until sometime later. Walker thought he could discipline Audrey, but dared Adrienne to touch Ariel. Adrienne couldn't help but think of Walker as an evil man for letting Ariel have her way all the time instead of helping her to teach Ariel right and wrong. But come to think of it, Ariel already knew what she was doing was wrong, that's why she got away with so much, because Walker let her. Adrienne couldn't blame Ariel because she was a child that needed to be taught right from wrong, so she didn't know any better. But Walker was the adult that knew better then to stand in the middle of a mother disciplining her child. Walker acted as though Ariel could do no wrong. Adrienne was going to spank Ariel because she had gotten tied of Ariel getting into stuff and getting away with it because she knew Walker wasn't going to let her mother discipline her, and it got to be a habit with Ariel doing stuff just to be doing it. Ariel had gotten a whole jar of Vaseline out of the closet and greased herself down with it from head to toe. Now Ariel waited just as good until her mother had washed and combed her hair. She went outside, took a bucket of dirt, and poured it over her head. Ariel was always into something because she knew her daddy wasn't going to let her mother discipline her so she thought. This one time, Adrienne fooled her and him. Ariel ran and jumped in her daddy's lap thinking that he would keep her mother from disciplining her, but Adrienne was ready for whatever happened that day. She went right on in the room behind Ariel with a switch in her hand. She whipped Ariel while she was in her daddy's lap. He got mad with Adrienne because she wrapped him too while she was at it. Adrienne got cursed out about it, but Walker didn't put his hands on her. Walker went as far as to put a gun to Adrienne's head since he couldn't beat on her anymore, threatening to blow her brains out. Daring her to say anything or to move. Everyday it was something with Walker and Ariel after she came into the world. Walker would leave the house on Saturday night after the girls and Adrienne came in from pastor's aide meeting at the church. Walker was dressed and on his way out the door as soon as Adrienne and the girls came in the house. Adrienne didn't stay for the committee meeting. But Walker pretended that was where he was going with his bible in his hand. Adrienne thought nothing of it, she really thought he was going to the committee meeting at the church. Adrienne thinking maybe he was finally trying to live right for a change. Adrienne had made up her mind to live for God and just assumed Walker was too. But from the way he treated Adrienne though, should have told her something wasn't right. Adrienne could feel something wasn't right in her body. She had little to no energy. It was like she was being drained of what energy she had left. She was all the time feeling sleepy sometimes sleeping too much, then other times she wasn't sleeping enough. It was to the point that she couldn't sleep at night, and by the time day came she couldn't get out of bed. She was late for work just about every morning after she was moved to the day shift at work. Being switch from the night shift back to the day shift had Adrienne's days and nights all messed up. She was so stressed out, depressed, everything and everyone got on her nerve. While taking medication for depression, Adrienne became even more depressed to the point she tried to take her own life by taking an over dose of pills. The pain in her body was very intense to the point She wasn't able to sit still for a long period of time during the day, and couldn't sleep at night. Adrienne knew something was wrong, but didn't know what it was at the time, nor did she know how to explain what was happening to her. Working at night wasn't agreeing with her at all. She had a routine of going to work, church, to the grocery store, and every blue moon to visit with some of her family members. Walker kept taps on her every move. He kept one step ahead of Adrienne, making sure of where she was at all times, so he would have time to run around in the streets with his mistress and to avoid running into Adrienne. So she *wouldn't see him and his mistress together* as it was him that was the one doing the cheating on her. But Walker made sure to tell other people that she was crazy. Adrienne didn't realize what was going on until word got to her that she was crazy, at lest that was what he was telling people. Adrienne didn't become crazy until she hit him over the head with that end table. She realized she was crazy for letting him beat on her all those years. He was telling people that Adrienne was cheating on him to cover-up what he himself was doing behind her back. Maybe she didn't know what he was doing behind her back, but God knew. For twelve years Adrienne put up with Walker and his craziness. She was good to him through it all, but that wasn't enough for him. He ended up walking away from the marriage because he no longer had control over Adrienne. By the time Adrienne's eyes were open to what he was doing and she was seeing things for herself, it was like everybody else knew already what he was doing. But Adrienne was the last to know. It was after the fact that people started telling Adrienne things about him and the woman he was cheating on her with. But they would beat around the bush when it came to the name of the woman. Telling her that the woman worked with her, and she drove a car like her. Adrienne was so ignorant to what was going on around her this was a different situation for her to go through. She think people were more so trying to find out her business then anything else or trying to find out how much she knew about the situation or if she was going to tell them something so they could run and tell someone else. But Adrienne didn't think it was a good idea to talk to people about her business. But even when she did talk to some one about something she would know whom she told and what she told them. Even when people didn't know her business they would think up some business about her to talk about.

Adrienne had a dream just before Walker walked off and left her. She dreamed Walker was having an affair with a woman that had a dark complexion. But the woman turned out to be light complexion. She even dreamed of falling from the top of a mountain, but woke up before hitting the bottom. Adrienne sure enough ended up having to walk away from her job for health reasons. She was at the breaking point. She felt she couldn't go on anymore. When the doctor asked her if her condition was job related, she didn't know how to answer because she didn't know what was wrong with her, so she told him no, instead of asking him what her condition was? Adrienne had no idea what was the cause of her condition. She had a hard time financially after that. But God blessed her to have a four-o-one k plan from her job. She had money going to the bank from her paycheck every week through her job. It wasn't much, but it kept the bills paid for a while having to budget every penny. Walker moved out of the house while Adrienne was in the hospital to be with his mistress. He wanted so much to hurt Adrienne even after all he had put her through already. He just made it worse. They promised each other earlier in the relationship that they would tell the other one if for some reason they decided not to continue in the relationship that they would let the other one know. Walker didn't do that, he wanted his cake and eat it too. Adrienne thought if anyone was going to leave the relationship it should have been her after all the hell he put her through.

Before Walker moved out, Adrienne talked to him about buying the house they were living in. With the rent they were paying they could have been paying on something of their own. He agreed. They both had good jobs. Walker worked for a chair company at night. Then he decided to go to a steel company. The house was across town they were leasing with the option to buy after two years. After living in the house for almost two years, Walker said to Adrienne that the people they were leasing the house from wanted four thousand dollars plus this brown Monte Carlo he had. Then they could start making the payments on the house as their own. They always went half on every thing they did.

Adrienne went to the bank and took out two thousand dollars. When they got to the lawyer's office to have the deeds written up and the house put over into both their names. Walker asked Adrienne for the money before they went into the lawyer office. But Walker wanted to go in and see the lawyer first to give him the money and he wanted Adrienne to wait until the lawyer drew up the deeds and all she had to do was come in and sign the deeds. Adrienne gave Walker the money thinking he was putting all the money together to give to the lawyer once inside. The deeds were going to be mailed to them after being filed with the courthouse. After the deeds came in the mail Adrienne notice all they had to pay was two thousand dollars, which she paid the whole amount.

Walker lied because he was in the process of moving out of the without telling Adrienne. She felt something wasn't right when he didn't want her to go into the lawyer office with him the first time. The papers were written up and all she had to do was sign the papers before they were to be sent to the courthouse. Adrienne was so drained, that she didn't even notice Walker had moved most of his things out of the house while she was in the hospital. He pretended to still be living in the house with them the reason she hadn't notice he had moved out. He had rented a room across town that Adrienne found out about by accident. While Adrienne was in the bed asleep, Walker would have his mistress to come to the house and pick him up. When Adrienne woke up the truck was in the yard, but Walker was nowhere to be found. By the time Walker knew Adrienne would be waking up, for some reason he had been in the woods Adrienne could tell from the sticky stuff on his clothes that he had been in the woods. Little by little he was removing his clothes from the house and pretended to be living in the room he had rented across town. But come to fine out the room was a cover up. He had moved in with his mistress. Adrienne was still cooking for him and everything as usual. It was a everyday routine for her. She get up in the morning after very little sleep, She would get the girls up for school, see to it that they got dressed while she was cooking their breakfast and his, then she would wait with them until the bus came. Then she would go back to bed for a few hours until it was time to cook dinner so Walker could have lunch to take to work with him, and the girls would have dinner when they came home from school. Adrienne was in the bed sleep, and Walker was only God knows where. Adrienne assumed that was how he had gotten his clothes out of the house without her knowing. The night he told her he was moving out, he had already taken all of his things even the air conditioner was gone out of the bed room window which they purchased together. By the time the girls came in from school it was time for Adrienne to go to work. While she was at work, Walker had time to do whatever he wanted since he got off work almost three hours before she did. Walker started an argument with Adrienne this was his way of getting around to telling her he had moved out of the house already. When she started asking him questions about his mistress, he'd get defensive about it by turning it around and asking her if she had ever seen him with a woman. No, but she caught him at her house which was where he was staying and using the room to make Adrienne think that was where he was staying. Adrienne caught him driving his mistress car. When Walker told her he had moved out already, he was sitting in his truck getting ready to pull out of the driveway. He then told her that they needed sometime apart. Adrienne let him know if he wanted to be with his mistress then to stay on out there with her. That was when he told her he was renting a room across town already. And that he would be back to get the rest of his things. Adrienne looked around the house for his things and the only thing he had left behind was a blue shirt. That was all she found of his in the house. He was hoping she would lose the house after he threatened to burn it down with her in it. The next day Adrienne was on her way to pay her water bill after she had gotten off work. The place where she paid her bill was across the street from where Walker was supposedly was staying. Adrienne decided she would go by to see if Walker was there. And to her surprise, Walker and his mistress were backing out of the driveway in his mistress car. That was why Adrienne never saw them together for one she wasn't looking, and two because him and his mistress would wait until it was dark outside thinking no one would see them. And just like Walker the windows were dark tint on his truck, the windows on her car were dark tint as well. Adrienne drove by the mistress house only to see Walker truck parked behind the woman house. Adrienne walked away from Walker several times because of his abuse. The abuse was so verbal, physical and emotional for Adrienne. She always felt sorry for Walker when he begged her to come back home. Promising her he wouldn't do it again and like a fool she went back every time. He made it a point to tell Adrienne she was nothing without him. And she wasn't going to find another man like him. And she prayed she would never find another man like him. A few weeks before Walker moved out he got mad and left the church because he wanted them to ordain him as a deacon in the church, and they didn't. There was another man and his family that joined the church, and they made him a deacon instead of Walker. The man was already a deacon from another church. This made Walker so mad he wanted Adrienne to leave her church and go with him to another church where he had joined. They were going to make him a deacon their, but Adrienne didn't think they knew enough about Walker to make him a deacon so soon after joining. The word said that a deacon is to be the husband of one wife. Adrienne was his second wife. Adrienne believed it was all about the money. They both had good paying jobs. Adrienne told Walker, she was not going to leave her home church just because he left out of anger. That made him even madder. After all she went through with him, then for him to turn around and leave her for another woman she wished she had left his ass a long time ago and never looked back the way she did her first husband.

But she stayed because she hoped things would some day get better when she should have praying instead. She wanted to keep the vows she had made to God and him for better or worse. Walker continued to make things worse as he made her out to be a bad mother. When all she tried to do was teach her children the way God said and prepare them for that great big world out their that we live in. So when they were ready to leave home they would know how to live on their own. Walker called the child abuse social workers on Adrienne accusing her of child abuse just because she whipped her own child. He only did that to get out of paying her child support. Even they took Walker side against Adrienne and the social worker was a member of their church. The social worker and Walker were in Sunday school class together. They somehow got together over lunch and made a case against Adrienne. It was years later, the social worker told Adrienne that she and Walker went out to lunch. The social worker went out to Adrienne's house along with two police officers. She didn't know what Walker told them but they came prepared to take her to jail. Adrienne was sitting at the bar between the living room and kitchen reading her bible when they showed up. Ariel slipped and called Walker after Adrienne wiped her with a switch for not cleaning her room like she asked her too. Ariel had been in her room all day long and the room looked the same as it did before her mother asked her to clean it up. Adrienne was all the time having to tell her more then one time to do something, and even then she didn't do what she was told. Ariel would get her cry on and Walker would tell her she didn't have to clean it up. The smell in the room would almost knock you out when you opened the door. Adrienne would go in and clean the room when she got tied of looking at it looking like a pig style long enough, just for Ariel to junk it up again which wasn't teaching her at all. The social worker said Ariel had a small wipe on her arm that disappeared the next day, and they wrote Adrienne up calling that child abuse. But Adrienne thought now where were they when she was being beaten with an extension cord? It didn't kill her, and she wasn't trying to kill Ariel. Adrienne was only doing what a mother is suppose to do when a child is disobedient. And that is put the rod on their backside. The Bible said spare the rod, spoil the child. And that was just what Walker did; spoiled the child. If Ariel hadn't tried to fight Adrienne while she was whipping her, she wouldn't had that whip on her arm, but that was what Walker told her to do, if her mother tried to whip her. Adrienne let the social worker and the officers in the house. She told them why she whipped Ariel then she let them into her room to see how it looked with all that junk everywhere compared to the rest of the house which was clean. Adrienne let them know that as long as Ariel lived in her house she was going to do as she was told or they could take her on with them and feed her. Then Adrienne thought they should of been around when she was growing up. She still had scares today from actually being abused, now that was child abuse back then.

Walker tried to have Adrienne put in jail once again when she caught him driving his mistress car, causing Adrienne to have to pay out money she didn't have for some bogus charges the two of them cooked up against her. But Adrienne had to bail him out of jail for hitting a handicap woman in a wheelchair while he was drunk. All Adrienne ever did was help him, and all he did was hurt her over and over again. She always sacrificed herself for everyone else, and wasn't appreciated for it. It was ignorance on her part not realizing all she had to do was pray to God and ask Him to help her in her situations. Adrienne didn't know then what to do like she know now. She thought she was loosing her mind as she went from doctor to doctor. She even tried to take her own life to make the pain attacking her body go away. But all she got was her stomach pumped, a few days in the hospital and a hospital bill. Adrienne had to agree to check herself into a mental institution before the doctor would release her from the hospital. Adrienne thought she knew what the Lord meant when He said not to be unequally yoked. To have her husband and child fighting against her was more then she could handle. Adrienne stayed two weeks in a mental institution. Walker came to see her but she didn't want to see him. She made up in her mind to let him go and let God. Adrienne was released to go back to work, but the pain started all over again. She had so much pain going on in her body that it was getting harder and harder for her to work. Her arm and hand was so painful and numb that she could hardly move them. Adrienne was back and fore to the doctor and taking medication. She couldn't sit still during the day, and couldn't sleep at night, the pain and numbness wasn't getting any better but worse as time went on. The side effects of the medication seemed to be worse then the pain. Adrienne realized the medications were causing other problems. She kept falling down for no reason at all. She thought at first her shoes were making her fall, but after falling for the fourth time over a period of time she knew something else was wrong. She realized she wasn't falling down before taking medication.

Adrienne knew falling down had to be one of the side effects of her medication. People that didn't know Walker the way Adrienne did thought he was a nice guy, but they only saw him on the outside dressed in a three piece suit that could be taken off and put back on at any time. Walker made superintendent of the Sunday school where they attended church. Adrienne couldn't understand why Walker even went to church because he wasn't doing what the Bible said do. He was doing just the opposite. He sang with the male chorus, but he wasn't singing to give God praise, it was to be seen by man. Walker' CB handle was filthy mc'nasty which he put on a tag on the front of his truck., and he was just that, filthy with a mc'nasty attitude, toward Adrienne anyway. He treated other people better then he treated her. He had other people fooled into thinking he was a nice guy. Walker being from the city and Adrienne was born and raised in the country. She didn't get out and around much she went only where she had too. Man looked at Walker outward appearance, while God was looking at his inside. He must not have known every time he put his hands on Adrienne it was like clapping God in the face. God gave him a good thing, and he abused her every chance he got. God said, that husbands were to love there wives as Christ loved the church, but Walker was an evil husband behind closed doors. Adrienne went through twelve long years of hell with him. She was too embarrassed scared and ashamed to tell or let anyone know what she was going through. It wasn't all that different from her childhood. She didn't talk back or fight back. She came to realize the devil was trying to kill her to keep her from getting to where God wanted her to be. Adrienne hid everything she was going through because of fear. She didn't think anyone cared about her anyway.

The more she tried to live right, and be a good person the more she was attacked by the devil through her husband and others around her. She loved Walker, and was good to him, but she didn't like his ways at all. Adrienne was that Proverbs thirty—one woman that took care of her family. She was a very nice person. Adrienne had a woman to tell her she was too nice. She didn't know what made the woman say that, but realized other people can see things we can't see for ourselves. Adrienne stayed in her marriage because she was afraid of being alone. Not realizing it was not healthy to stay in an abusive marriage. Adrienne wanted so much for Walker to be a good husband, and father, but she should have been asking God for a saved husband and man of God instead of just a husband. She was giving Walker a chance to do right. And he just refused to do so. He ended up leaving her in the end after all he had put her through just to hurt her some more for another woman. Walker mistress left her husband to be with him. Adrienne could have dated the other woman husband if she wanted too. He asked Adrienne too, but she didn't want too. She wasn't going to do evil for evil the way some people do, there were children involved and she couldn't do that to them. On Sunday mornings Walker pretended to be holier then thou, and when church was over the real him came out, it was like he was processed. He showed man what he wanted them to see, and showed Adrienne who he really was, a jealous, abusive, loud talking, controlling, arrogant, intimidating alcoholic, keeping Adrienne isolated from her family. She already didn't have any friends that she could hang out with she couldn't trust anyone. Walker turned out to be a liar and a cheater who didn't care who he hurt to get his way. Walker left home and moved in with his mistress and pretended to rent a room across town as a way to try and keep Adrienne from seeing him as the adulterer he really was. Walker was at his mistress house more then at the room he was suppose to be living in. Adrienne just so happen to drive by Walker mistress house only to find Walker truck parked behind her house after one day of him moving out from his family. Adrienne didn't like having to start all over again about as much as she didn't like being alone. But she decided she was going to live alone in peace after all the hell Walker had put her through, and it was worth it to be free of him, and his abuse. Once again Adrienne fail into a deep depression while experiencing pain and numbness on the right side of her upper body and lower back. It seemed as though everything and everybody was against her at the same time. She was in bad shape after suffering a breakdown. She was admitted into a mental institution for the second time for several weeks. For the first three days She didn't know she was in the world. After waking up from a deep sleep which was much needed. Adrienne's face and eyes were all swollen from sleeping in her contact lens. Adrienne's contacts were not meant to sleep in. but she had no idea the medication was going to make her sleep so long. She was so out of it that she wasn't responding to the doctor, so she was put on a different floor with patients that walked around in a daze talking to themselves and out of there minds. Adrienne looked around and began to ask God how did she get there? She began to pray asking God to help her out of this place. Adrienne couldn't understand how she came all the way from being a Sunday school teacher to being in that place? Before the day was over Adrienne was put back into her private room were she had been before. She began to praise God for answering her prayer so soon after she prayed. Adrienne still didn't understand what was happening to her. Pain was coming from every where and nobody bothered to tell her what was going on with her. Adrienne found a bible in one of the drawers in her room. She opened it up and began to read it. It was such a comfort to her. Psalms her favorite book of the bible, the twenty—third numbers. The Lord is my Shepherd.

Adrienne felt so much better then she had in a long time. She started to read and study her bible every day after that and found that there was a lot she didn't know about God and His Son Jesus. Once again Adrienne was released to go back to work. The pain and numbness started all over again from her neck to her fingertips on the right side of her upper body. The pain was very painful, sensitive and numb at the same time. It got so bad she couldn't use her right hand anymore for the pain. She wasn't even making production anymore on her job. That should have told her supervisors something was wrong with her. For her not to make production, something was terribly wrong. She reported it to her supervisor after going to the doctor that she wasn't suppose to lift more then fourteen pounds, but she stated that they didn't have any thing for her to do that would be fourteen pounds. Adrienne left the job and went home. Her bills started falling behind, her check was being garnished, the house was being foreclosed on and the car was reprocessed. Everyone was looking at Adrienne all crazy as though she had done something wrong. The devil had sat her up to fail, but she give Glory to God for He carried her through it all.

Adrienne's daughter Audrey was about to graduate high school, and there was no income coming in to help with the things needed to be done. It had been over a year since Adrienne signed up for she disability from her job. The money she had in the bank was going fast. She budgeted ever penny so she could pay bills each month. Adrienne had to file bankruptcy in order to keep the house from going into foreclosure and procession of the car. God made a way out of no way for them. Adrienne had a four-o-one k plan check to come in the mail from her job. She was a nervous rack by that time. It was a long time coming, but God sent it right on time. Audrey needed money for her class ring, invitations, pictures and things for her graduation. She was crowned homecoming queen too that year. God did it all for them. Adrienne had no idea where her next penny was coming from. She continued to pray and thank God. She heard a knock at the door, it was the constable with divorce papers from Walker. He filed for a divorce to be with his mistress. Adrienne should have been the one to file for a divorce from him. Walker claimed to have pictures of Adrienne with another man, but if that were the case, it was after the fact that she caught him at his woman's house. The two of them would wait until it was dark thinking no one would see them and she would go and pick him up leaving his truck where he was renting a room or Walker would park his truck behind her house. They moved into an all white neighborhood across town. It was devastating at first for Adrienne to see the two of them together, but as time went by, it got easier for her to let go and let God.

After all Walker had put her through enough. The day she signed those divorce papers was a big relief for her. She was free from hell. Adrienne felt sorry for Walker after giving him the divorce he wanted instead of fighting it. She didn't want to drag all of their business into court. To think about it that was just what she should have done exposed him for whom he really was and people would have known just what kind of person he was. But the fact that God knew was good enough for her. God's word said to fret not thyself because of evildoers, but trust in the Lord and do good to them that hate you. That was all Adrienne ever did to others was good only to get hatred from them in return. Some people may call it being weak, but she called it treating people the way she want to be treated. Walker tried to make things as hard as he could for Adrienne telling whom ever would listen that she was cheating on him. When all the time it was him that was following her around driving another woman car. The windows on Dorothy car was tinted very dark. Walker thought no one would be able to see him driving her car. But Adrienne came face to face with him one day just as she was getting out of her car for an appointment with her attorney. She stepped out her car just in time to turn around and look right in Walker face driving his mistress car. He was in such shock that Adrienne saw him that he tried to back the car up on a one way street. But cars were behind him and the light was on red in front of him so he had nowhere to go but forward after the light changed. Adrienne got back in her car and followed behind him only to catch him at the red light where they were down through town. Walker had nowhere else to go so he pulled off the road at the last gas station at the end of town. Adrienne pulled in behind him, she gets out of her car and started beating on him the way he use to beat on her. That was something she never would have done, but the thought that he had been lying to her all the time about Dorothy his mistress. Adrienne lost it for a moment and didn't realize Walker had stuck his cigarette to her between the neck and shoulder. Walker had a cigarette in his hand when she walked upon him. It wasn't until she woke up three days later back in the mental institution that she noticed he had burned her. Someone at the gas station where they were called the police. When the police got there they immediately handcuffed Adrienne and put her in the back of the police car. She couldn't hear what Walker told them, but they let him go and Adrienne was taken to the police station. Adrienne had both of her children with her at the police station while Walker was off doing only God knows what. Adrienne had to pay twenty dollars in order to be released from the police station. For some reason the police took Walker side against her even though he was in the wrong, following her around in another woman car. Adrienne realized she was in the wrong too, but Walker thought just because he was a mason he could get away with whatever he wanted. There was some kind of hand sign he gave the police officer. Whatever Walker said to the officer he believed for him to just let him go. Once again making Adrienne out to be the bad person. She had no trust in the police or anyone else for that matter after that. Adrienne had a hard time under standing why in the public eye Walker pretended to be this good loving husband? But treated her like dirty behind closed doors. The monster in him came out when they were behind closed doors. The fact that Dorothy left her own husband to sneak around with her husband Adrienne couldn't understand. Then she thought, maybe it wasn't for her to understand. But as soon as Adrienne signed the divorce papers two weeks after the divorce was final, Walker and Dorothy were married. Still Walker continued to meddle in Adrienne life about their daughter Ariel. Adrienne decided she wasn't going to take it anymore. So she let Ariel go and live with Walker and his new wife.

Adrienne decided to go to college since she had a lot of time on her hands. Her oldest daughter was getting ready to start college and Adrienne thought she always wanted to go to college so this was a great opportunity for her to go to college too. After Adrienne graduate, she was offered a job working in a nursing home as a hair stylist, which was her major in cosmetology. She did more visiting with the people in the nursing home then she did hair. It was a blessing for Adrienne to get to know people, she thought, they were in worse shape then she was. They loved for Adrienne to come and just talk with them. Adrienne was visiting this lady in the nursing home. Adrienne had no idea who this lady was and every week or whatever days she worked she would go by to see the woman. Adrienne had gotten so attacked to the woman she would comb her hair in the room because the woman was bed written. She was suppose to do the people hair that were able to go to the beauty shop but Adrienne had compassion in her heart for others. Adrienne would sit with the woman, whatever she needed for her to do and never charged her anything. After three years of visiting with the lady, Adrienne ran into Dorothy in the hallway of the nursing home as she was on her way to visit the lady. Dorothy was coming out of the lady's room. Adrienne spoke to her and they started to talk in the hallway. Dorothy said to Adrienne that the woman she was visiting was her aunt. After all that time Adrienne had never seen Dorothy visit her aunt. Adrienne realized she was on a mission from the Lord to visit the sick and shut in so it didn't matter to her that the lady was Dorothy's aunt. Adrienne continued to visit the lady until she died. She had gotten just that close to her. It was God in Adrienne for her to continue on the way she did.

Walker died a few years later, after his stepson beat his ass, putting him in the hospital. He was already dying of lung cancer. The word says you weep what you sow. Walker' stepson and Ariel were in the same carat class together. Walker wanted her to take carat so she could jump on Adrienne if she tried to whip her. But he didn't know what goes around comes around and it came right back around to Walker getting the whipping that ended his life sooner then he thought. Dorothy may have gotten everything that should have been Adrienne and her daughter's, but then again Adrienne thought she can have it. It's only material stuff. But what God has for me, it is for me. Adrienne thought she rather have Jesus. The Word said, Seek ye first the kingdom of God and everything else will be added unto you. Adrienne asked the Lord for strength to go on in the name of Jesus until her time come that He will call her home. Adrienne realized she don't have to be sad, but be encouraged, as she encourage herself in the Lord. Before Walker died, he called Adrienne and asked her to forgive him. She did because she wanted God to forgive her for her sins as well.

At the age of forty, the Lord blessed Adrienne with her house and car paid for, she was debt free. The same house that was to be foreclosed on and the same car man reprocessed. They are material things, but God blessed her to burrow them for a little while longer. It all belongs to Him. Adrienne thanked God that He kept her through it all. The Lord blessed her as she started to have faith in Him. He made a way out of no way for her and her children. She thank God for making her strong enough to take it!

CHAPTER THREE

Adrienne went on trying to put the pieces of her life back together again. Only to run into a man she thought was her husband. He was a guy she had a crush on in high school. But he never knew it. She thought this was fate running into him after all those years and maybe it was suppose to be. Things had finally come through with Adrienne's disability and she could breathe a little better financially. She sat out one morning in search of getting the tires on her car rotated and balanced. She drove up to this place that sold and fixed tires and thought she would get them to rotate the tires for her and their he was. As they greeted one another with a hello long time no see. They started to talk about the old school days. Before Adrienne could leave the place, Mark asked her, if she wouldn't mind going out to dinner with him. Adrienne really didn't want to be bothered so she hesitated. She explained to him she had just come out of a bad relationship and wasn't ready to date anyone else at that time. He went on to convince her that it was only dinner, no strings attached. Adrienne then thought to herself, why not it's just dinner? She excepted, but later wish she hadn't after he called her to confirm the dinner date and to tell her he didn't have a car, so Mark invited her to his house for dinner. A light went off in her head but she decided she wasn't going to let her other relationships block her from going on with her life. Besides it was just dinner. Adrienne was sucked in almost immediately by his charming ways after she got to his place. He knew just what to say to impress her and to make her laugh, which was something she hadn't done in a long time. What Adrienne didn't know was the reason behind it all. He turned out to be the type of person that could charm you out of anything that would benefit him. Adrienne noticed he lived in a nice brick house when she got there it was very neat for a man, she thought. That was even more impressive to her that he would invite her over to his place for dinner instead of going to a restaurant. When she got there the lights were down, music playing softly, candles lit, everything was so romantic and smelling good. It just sat the mood for whatever as they sat across the table from one another talking, while the food was slowly cooking. Mark handed Adrienne what she thought was a cigarette since he smoked and so did she at the time and had for years. The reason why she thought it was a cigarette he passed it over to Adrienne as she took a puff of it. She could tell that it wasn't a cigarette but marijuana. A complete calmness came over her in a way that she had never felt before. She felt very relaxed as though nothing or no one could hurt her again, but she was wrong. This man kept on telling her lie after lie to cover up the first lie he told to get what he wanted. The lies were so convincing that even he thought they were true. That was just how good he was at lying. But it took Adrienne a little while before she realized just how big of a liar he really was. She couldn't see that they were lies until things just weren't adding up to what he was saying to her, and his lies started to catch up to him. After months of getting so deeply involved with him. Mark told Adrienne he was getting kicked out of his house, and he didn't have any place to live. This was another trick of the devil. But what he didn't tell her was he had stopped paying his rent and had to move out. Adrienne believed it was his intentions all along to move in with her the reason why he stopped paying his rent. She told him he needed to go and stay at his mother's house because she wasn't comfortable letting him move in the house with her and they were not married. Then he claimed there were already to many people staying in his mother's house. Adrienne being the kind hearted person that she was felt sorry for him. She gave in letting him stay in the house with her until he could find somewhere else to stay. But that day didn't came when he would find some place else to stay. It wasn't long after Mark moved in that he asked Adrienne to marry him. Things were happening too fast for Adrienne. But she excepted the proposal not realizing until after they were married and all of his lies started coming together. It was all in his plan from the start to move in with Adrienne. She found out right after they were married that he really did stop paying his rent the reason why he had to move out of the house. But he told Adrienne that the lady he was renting the house from was going to sell the house, so he had to move. He had Adrienne fooled right up until after they were married. Things changed, too bad Adrienne couldn't see him for who he really was before she married him. Everything started to go down hill from there so did

Adrienne's bank account with one lie after the other. Mark claimed to have been fired from his job, and for some reason he couldn't draw his unemployment. At lest that was what he told Adrienne, but his plan all along was for Adrienne to take care of him. There was a lack of communication going on between the two of them. Instead of Mark talking to Adrienne truthfully about what was going on with him, he kept lying. Mark's plan was since Adrienne was on disability at the time. He would pretend to get kicked out of the house he was living in, move in with Adrienne, quit his job, so Adrienne could take care of him and he wouldn't have to pay his child support for eight children. But that wasn't in Adrienne's plan. She believed Mark was the reason that they cut her off of her disability because she married him. By Mark not having a car, Adrienne would let him use her car to go out and look for him another job. Everyday it was one excuse after the other. Mark would be gone all day as though he'd been out looking for a job, only God knows where he was and what he was doing. But word got back to Adrienne that Mark was not looking for job, but was riding around all day in her car with other people in the car. Since he would be gone all day and still came back without a job, Adrienne decided she would take him to look for a job herself some where she knew they would be hiring everyday. And beside, she needed to have a way to get to her doctor's appointments without having to wait for him to bring the car back each day. The first day that she took him looking for a job, he was scheduled for orientation that same day. He was to return for work the next day. That let Adrienne know he wasn't looking for a job. But what he was doing was hanging out with his friends smoking pot and laying up with whoever she was. Mark thought Adrienne didn't know about his women friends. Whoever she was, was bowl enough to call the house and ask for him by name. Adrienne took Mark back and forth to work for a while until she felt she was no longer up to making the trip. Going out everyday was exhausting and draining her fast of energy. Along with the medications she was taking, she didn't want to risk falling asleep while driving. So Adrienne decided to let him drive the car again to work. And come to find out, he wasn't even going to work at all. Either that or his whole check went toward child support. All Adrienne know is he would leave the house every morning as if he was going to work, but on Friday he didn't have a paycheck to prove he had been going to work. He was doing things that a con man would do, like he went to Adrienne's bank and ask for money from her account without asking her first knowing the money in her account wasn't his. While at the same time, he was telling Adrienne he was putting money into her checking account each week after he'd cash his check. Each week Adrienne was writing checks to pay the bills or buy grocery, and before she knew anything the checks were coming back as insufficient funds. There was no money in the checking account, and there was a twenty-dollar charge for each check that was returned. Adrienne ended up paying out well over six hundred dollars because of his lies and conning ways. She didn't even have the money to pay the car note. She woke up one morning and the car was gone. She thought someone had stolen the car so she called the police, and were she had purchased the car only to find out the car had been reprocessed again. Adrienne had to file bankruptcy again just to keep them from selling the car and foreclosing on the house. But before she could get money to pay a lawyer to file bankruptcy, she had to wait until she got another paycheck the next month. Adrienne traveled all night on a bus to Nashville Tennessee to retrieve the car back that was taken from her yard in the night. Then she drove all the way back home by herself after having to stop and at times to rest. She had no idea where she was, so she just drove. She stopped to get a map to put her on the road home, reading the signs the best she could, and she prayed that the Lord would see her safely back home as she prayed all the way home. Adrienne had no idea how many miles she went out of the way to get home, but when she saw a sign that said Michigan, she praised God all the way home. Mark went as far as to talk Adrienne's grandmother out of letting him borrow her power saw, and six or more hundred dollars with no intentions of paying her back. He never told Adrienne he had borrowed money from her grandmother, only the power saw. It was some months later Adrienne stopped by to see her grandmother and her grandmother asked her about Mark. Adrienne told her grandmother they were no longer together. That was when she grandmother told Adrienne she had let Mark borrow the power saw and six hundred or so dollars. Adrienne could not believe what she was hearing, that this man would go to her grandmother and ask her for money without telling her. Adrienne's grandmother had taken out a loan from the bank for the money she gave him with the agreement that he would make the payments on the loan each month and he wasn't paying the notes the way he told her he would do. Mark conned Adrienne's grandmother telling her he needed the money for Adrienne. But Adrienne had no idea he had gotten money from her grandmother until her grandmother told her. Adrienne was furious that her grandmother would give Mark that kind of money without talking to her first. Adrienne never saw the money, nor did he tell her anything about the money. If it hadn't been for Adrienne's grandmother, she never would have known he asked her grandmother for money and she gave it to him. Adrienne was at the end of her ropes with him, and she just couldn't deal with him and his lies anymore. Adrienne paid her grandmother back two-hundred dollars and Mark was suppose to pay her the rest of it after he talked Adrienne into letting him file her on his income tax. He was suppose to give Adrienne eight hundred dollars so she could pay her grandmother back what he old her. After he got his income tax check, he couldn't get it cashed so he asked Adrienne to cash it for him. Adrienne already had an account at the bank and he didn't, so she had the check cashed for him. And instead of Adrienne taking out the money he was going to give her for her grandmother, she gave it all to him thinking he was going to do the right thing and do what he said he would do. But she was wrong, he gave her two hundred dollars and that was what she gave to her grandmother. Adrienne put the rest in God's hand. After that, Adrienne's grandmother sent Noel, a second cousin of her to get the power saw because he had wanted to borrow it. So Adrienne told him to go out to the shed to get the saw. Noel came back into the house saying that he couldn't find it. Adrienne went out to shed to look for it knowing that was where she put the power saw. And she couldn't find it. She knew she had put it in the shed herself and locked the door. Mark had taken the saw without her knowing and it was nowhere to be found. Adrienne went back out to the shed and looked once again after Noel had left. Adrienne knew she had put her grandmother's power saw in the shed after Mark and she used it to cut down trees in the back yard. The shed was locked still, so Adrienne knew it had to of been Mark that took it. It was her guess that he took it to exchange for pot, sold or pawned it but it was nowhere to be found.

Before realizing she just didn't want to put up with him anymore, he continued on with his lies as he then went to the next door neighbor's house and talked them out of using one of their cars. This was during the time Adrienne's car had been reprocessed. Mark kept the neighbor car for she didn't know how long, but confusion came up about the car with the people next door. Adrienne had no idea what was going on with that, but she think Mark kept the car longer then he should. Their was a like in communication, she asked Mark to leave her home, and as he was leaving. The car either stopped on the side of the road, or he left it on purpose. All the conning, the lies, and the cheating, Adrienne couldn't deal with it anymore. She asked him to leave and she wanted a divorce. He wasn't trying to do better. But added problems on top of problems. Adrienne continued going church, it was a revival night and the preacher preached about forgiveness. Adrienne felt the Lord was talking to her telling her she needed to forgive her husband, so after church she decided to go by his mother's house were he was suppose to be staying. She thought maybe they could talk and come to some kind of understanding. But he wasn't there. Mark's brother told Adrienne he was at a house around the corner. Adrienne drove up to the house and blew the horn. After a few minutes a woman came out of the house with her housecoat open in the front as though she had just put it on showing her bra and panties. She walked up to the car to see who it was. Adrienne asked the woman if Mark was there? And she said he was. Adrienne asked if she could see him? The woman turned going back into the house to get him. Adrienne waited for him to come out of the house. It took him a long time to come out of the house. As though he knew it was Adrienne or maybe he had to get into his clothes first. Or he had to think of what lie he was going tell her this time. When he did come out of the house, there it was a lie so big that only he believed it was true. Even though Adrienne was stunted by what she had just seen. She thought maybe this was a blessing and this was meant for her to see just what kind of man he really was. Now she wouldn't feel bad about divorcing him, and she could move on with her life once again. Mark then tried to call Adrienne on the phone with more lies, telling her that he loved her and he wanted them to get back together. Mark went on to tell Adrienne that the woman house he was at, there was nothing going on between them. That he use to date the woman sister, who was in prison. Adrienne asked him if that was the case, why would the woman be walking around in front of him showing her bra and panties? He couldn't answer that. But like a fool Adrienne believed him, and took him back once again thinking he had changed. Then to she needed him to help out around the house with things she was no longer able to do.

Like the yard work and stuff he was good at that. But still he hadn't changed at all. He asked Adrienne if he could use her car to go to his mother's house and he'd be right back. It was early the next morning when Mark returned with some lame excuse that he had fallen asleep. That was the last straw with Adrienne because after all that time with him she knew him. A player he was so she asked him for a divorce once again. But he wouldn't sign the divorce papers, so she had to trick him into signing them. This time there was no going back. Adrienne asked him one day who he was living for? And he said to her if Jesus is on the right hand of God, then who sit on the other? And that let her know that the devil is his daddy.

It was income tax time and Mark's W-2 forms came in the mail at Adrienne's mailing address. Adrienne called him on the phone to let him know that they had come to her address and the only way he was going to get them was that he signed the divorce papers. It took him a long time to do so but in that time Adrienne decided to go to college and take up a coarse in English comp one hoping to improve her comprehension which was a struggle in her life not being able to comprehend some things very well. She was slow at comprehending. Also she took a coarse in philosophy. She wanted to learn more about God and our Lord and Savior Jesus Christ. And what she could do to better herself from all the disappointments.

While at the same time she was doing some volunteer work at her cousin Charlie's tax office. She just wanted something to do to keep her mind off of her problems. For some reason she was taken off of her disability. She didn't know if it was because she went to college, or maybe because social security thought she was able to work, or because she had gotten married, but the pain in her body was still there. And getting worse, but she tried to cope with it the best she could. Even though she couldn't understand what was causing all the pain. So many things were going on, and she didn't know how to explain it to her doctor what was going on with her. She just knew she was stuff, sore and sensitive at times. But something was finding a job wasn't easy after being on disability. But after the semester of college was over she then decided she wanted to make something of herself, so she stepped out on faith and went back to college to get a degree in Cosmetology something she always wanted to be was a hair stylist. It was always her dream to have her own business, and with God's help, she went on to make that dream come true. She attended East Wood Community College closer to home so she wouldn't have to live on campus. She received the Student of the Month Award. She made the President's Scholar list and received the Vocational Student of the Year Award. Saving up her money while in college Adrienne began to shop around for some of the things she would need to put in her salon. There was a hair salon in Philadelphia Michigan, one of the ladies she attended cosmetology with told her about. It was going out of business, so she purchased what she could with what money she had, one hair dryer, two dryer chairs, a shampoo bowl and chair, and a styling chair, storing them away until they were needed. So after graduating college in nineteen- ninety- seven with honors, and at the top of her class. Adrienne used the grant money she received and purchased a storage building to use as her salon. Little by little she would buy some of the things she was going to need to make it look like a salon inside. She started with putting in paneling for the walls and ceiling, sectioning off a place for the bathroom, hot water tank, shelves, cabinets, mirrors, towels, and had the plumbing installed, until everything was into place. It took her three years to get the shop up and running, but she thank God for being God.

While in college Adrienne met and married husband number four, Antonio. She brought her storage building in his name so he could establish his own credit to buy him a car. It was Antonio, his dad and uncle that put the paneling in the salon, and blocked off an area for the bathroom. But before they could finish all the work that needed to be done in the shop, Antonio was put in jail. He was then sent back to Florida where he had skipped out on his probation officer. The devil tried really hard to block Adrienne's progress, making it difficult for her to get the work finished on the shop. But she refused to give up after coming so far. She had to hire people to come in and finish the work with the help of God and her brother who knew a guy that did the kind of work she needed done. The guy that Adrienne's brother had working on the shop wanted to get paid before the job was finished. He liked to drink beer or whatever while he worked. But Adrienne knew he wouldn't get finished if she paid him before the work was completed. Adrienne ended up having to hire someone else. Although it took three years before she could get the work finished on the shop, God did it for her. The name of the business was More Hair and nails Salon, opened March eighth of year two thousand. That was a blessed day for her. Well the first most blessed day was when she found Jesus, and He saved her. She thanked God for her children and grandchildren, then the business. She thank God so dear for her life, because she knew it could have been worse, so she thank God for as well as it is, because she know that, if it had not been for the Lord, who was on her side, where would she be. Adrienne thanked God for His deliverance and for His Grace and Mercy.

CHAPTER FOUR

———————

Antonio and Adrienne met when on a blind date with her sister and her friend. They all were going out to dinner and a movie. The evening turned out to be quite fun. After meeting Antonio, Adrienne thought he was cute, nicely build, with cold black hair. She didn't quite know what to say to Antonio, he was a white Cuban. And the guy her sister's friend was a black Cuban who knew very little English. But Antonio spoke English very well. He acted as though he knew Adrienne already, he wasn't shy at all. Once the date ended, Adrienne decided she wasn't going to see him anymore, but to her surprise, Antonio showed up at the tax office where she was one day. After she had told him she wasn't going to see him anymore. Adrienne thought it was sweet of him to come looking for her. She was feeling kind of uncomfortable dating outside of her race. But they didn't see color, just human beings. If only it was that way with every race. Antonio convinced Adrienne to change her mind about dating him. They started to see each other on a regular basis. Mostly on the weekend, Antonio had a job and that was quite a distance away. But he didn't have a car. He was working on getting one. That was another reason why Adrienne decided she didn't want to see him anymore. She had been through that not having a car with her third husband. Antonio would call her everyday wanting to know what she was doing? Then he would want her to come and pick him up on the weekend. Things were moving a little to fast for Adrienne. She felt he was smothering her. She was still in college when they got together. It wasn't long that he asked her to marry him. And he wasn't taking no for an answer. Adrienne finally said yes. Antonio was there to see her graduate from college. Adrienne couldn't help but feel something strange was going on with Antonio. He lived in this house with several other people. One thing about them they knew how to live together in one house until it was time for them to go to work. They saved their money to get what they wanted. Antonio and Adrienne went shopping one day in the mall. While looking around Antonio decided he wanted to buy car phones. He was trying to establish his own credit, so he used the credit card he had gotten in the mail. But the lady behind the counter said to him that the name and social security number on the card didn't match. But some kind of way Antonio was able to get the phones. He then brought later on a computer and hooked everything up. He was very smart when it came to electronics. But Adrienne thought she could have done without the car phone. She couldn't go anywhere without Antonio calling her, not even to the grocery store without him calling before she could make it to the store and she would be just done left home. Antonio was very hyper and Adrienne was a nervous wreck around him. He was like a leach and Adrienne didn't like for him touching on her all the time. She finally got to meet his dad and his uncle. They didn't speak any English at all. Antonio had to interpret for them, and Adrienne couldn't stand when the three of them got together. They talked so fast and she couldn't understand what they were saying. It was nerve wrecking they could have been talking about her for all she know. For some reason Antonio kept pressuring Adrienne to marry him. Adrienne kept feeling something wasn't right she couldn't figure it out until after they were married. Soon after they were married Antonio started to change. He had told her he wouldn't be so hyper once they were married. But that didn't change at all, look like he got worse. Antonio had finally purchased a car. Adrienne was so glad he could drive to see her instead of her going to get him every weekend. As Adrienne and Antonio traveled to Montgomery one day, Antonio was having trouble with his car. The clutch was going out on the car. And he was going to have to leave the car over night for them to work on it the next day. So as they were driving down the interstate Antonio moved to the right shoulder of the road all of a sudden without giving Adrienne any kind of warning he was going to pull to the side of the road.

Adrienne was driving in her car behind him. She looked up in her rear view mirror just in time to see a big eighteen wheeler coming fast right on her bumper. She called out the name Jesus and God directed her to speed up, turn on her signal light and then move to the right of the road. God delivered her from a situation that could have taken her life. She thanked God and looked around to find herself a ways down the road from where Antonio was. Antonio claimed the car stopped on him. But he was a really bad driver anyway. Adrienne didn't go to many places with him driving unless she drove herself. Adrienne thought about the fact that she had taken out some life insurance on herself leaving Antonio and her children as the beneficiary. Adrienne wondered, if Antonio hadn't pulled off to the side of the road on purpose trying to get her killed for the insurance money. She gave God Glory for saving her life that day.

Adrienne's daughter Ariel decided she wanted to move back in the house with her after things didn't work out with her dad Rick and his new wife the way she thought it would. Adrienne said to Rick, she would let Ariel live with him only if he would let her come back home if she wanted too. But Rick did everything he could to keep from paying Adrienne spousal and child support. Ariel had to write a letter telling Adrienne she wanted to come home and her daddy wouldn't let her. Adrienne called Rick. He got really nasty on the phone. So Adrienne said to him she was going to get a lawyer and let them settle things. The way she wished she had done in the divorce case. But she didn't fight it. She gave it over to God.

Antonio really began to act crazy after Ariel moved back in the house with her mother. He acted as if he didn't want Ariel there with them. What he fell to realize was, Ariel was Adrienne's child and that was her home before it became his. One morning Adrienne got up to fix breakfast. Antonio decided he wanted to go and visit with his dad and uncle. Adrienne sensed something was going on Antonio wasn't telling her about. He asked Adrienne if she would leave his breakfast in the microwave until he got back, which she did. Adrienne's dad had been in the hospital having goal bladder surgery. When he was released from the hospital Adrienne decided to take her dad home with her until he recovered so she could make sure he took his medication the way he was suppose too. Antonio became jealous of the fact, he thought Adrienne was giving her dad more attention then she was giving him. Antonio always got really mad when something or someone got more of her attention then he did. After Antonio returned from seeing his dad and uncle, he come in the house and took his plate from the microwave throwing his food on the floor, missing the garbage can. He claimed it was because he only had three pieces of bacon on his plate. Which was what she had fixed for everyone in the house was three pieces of bacon each. Adrienne had gotten fed up with him and his bad attitude.

Adrienne's dad didn't want to get in the middle of things so he left and went home to his house because of the way Antonio was acting. That made Adrienne angry that he would show his behind around other people the way he did. Adrienne asked Antonio to leave her home. He left, but kept calling her to come back. She decided she would give him something to think about for a few days before she finally let him come back. Adrienne was already hurting in her body and his craziness didn't make her feel any better.

It was Memorial Day weekend and all the family was planning to come together. Everyone was going to meet up at Adrienne's dad house. It was early evening when the phone rang it was one of Adrienne's cousins. He was on the police force. He said to Adrienne he needed for her sister, her brother and herself to come to her dad's house. It was an emergency. Adrienne immediately thought something had happened to her dad since she couldn't get her cousin to tell her anything over the phone. Adrienne quickly showered and got dressed. When she got to her dad's house the yard was filled with cars. She didn't think much about that since it was the day they usually had family reunion anyway. As she got out of the car, she could see people were sitting on the front porch of her sister's house. Which was next door to her dad's house. As she walked over to the house she could see her dad sitting there on the porch with his head down. No one was saying anything. Adrienne walked up to her dad and asked him what was going on. Her dad said to her that her stepmother and her two half sisters were killed in a car accident that morning. Adrienne couldn't say anything but felt sorry for her dad. After Adrienne hugged her dad's neck to comfort him, she then asked him what happened. He said to her they were hit by a log truck. Then he said to her he was suppose to have gone with them. But he was tied and wasn't feeling to good. So Adrienne's dad decided he wouldn't go with them on the trip. Adrienne was glad he didn't go with them, then that would have been four family members to die in one day instead of three. The next few days, Adrienne went with her dad to the funeral home to take care of the necessary arrangements. Adrienne had her cosmetology licenses so she volunteered to do the hair and makeup of Hanna and her two sisters to cut down on the cost of the funeral. Adrienne had gone with a friend of hers whom hair salon she started out working in to do the hair of a woman who had passed. She knew God was preparing her for the time when she was going to have to do it by herself. Adrienne knew doing a dead person hair and makeup was too hard for her. But no one else knew it but God. Adrienne never liked going to funerals or funeral homes, but that was a part of doing hair as well. And somebody had to be strong for the family, so she asked God to give her strength to do what she had to do. God gave her the strength to step up and do what had to be done for the family. Just before the funeral Adrienne's dad wanted her to go to the funeral home and fix his baby girls hair the way she wore her hair all the time with a bang to cover her forehead. To be in a room along with three dead bodies gave Adrienne the chills. But once again she asked God to give her strength to do what she needed to do. After all Adrienne had to endure she felt all along. No one knew what she was going through. Adrienne couldn't get her husband Antonio to go with her to the funeral, he didn't like going to funerals he said, every since his grandmother passed away. It was hard enough getting him to go to church, he said they stayed in church to long for him. He was Catholic and Adrienne was Baptist. She got him to go to church with her a few times. They even got married in the church. She tried to get him to read the bible with her, but he didn't want to read it until something went wrong. Then he would pick it up to read.

It was Adrienne's birthday, the best day she had had in a long time. Antonio had finally done something to make her happy for her birthday. She felt a peaceful feeling come over her. The next day as Antonio was on his way home from work. He said he ran into a cousin of Adrienne on the interstate and decided to race with him. And he got pulled over by the police, but her cousin was on the police force. So she didn't know what happened. He could have been trying to out run the police for all she know. Antonio said, he was pulled over and they ran his licenses and name. The police took him straight to jail. Adrienne thinks Antonio knew they were looking for him the reason he had to go to Florida with his dad and uncle. There was a warrant out for his arrest. And he didn't bother to tell Adrienne about it. A few weeks before Antonio was arrested, Antonio, his dad, and uncle all went to Florida where they lived before coming to live in Montgomery. Antonio said to Adrienne, he needed to go and take care of some business and see his children while he was there. He said he had two twin boys. Once they returned, Antonio went on to tell Adrienne things in bits and pieces, like the reason why he was in prison was because he had taken something that didn't belong to him. He was on patrol. He never told her they were looking for him until that day he called her from the jail saying they were taking him back to Florida. Adrienne wasn't able to see him until that Sunday during visiting hour. She went to the jail that same night thinking she was going to bond him out. But there was something he wasn't telling her for him to have to go back to Florida. Adrienne continued to press her way to get to church. She went to church that Sunday morning. After church the choir had to go to another church in the same county Antonio was in jail. The pastor was to preach there. After the choir song Adrienne left in order to get to the jail on time for visiting hour. She had no idea what was going on or who she was married too. She felt sorry for him because everything he was telling her sounded like a lie. Adrienne was more confused then ever. A few days later, Adrienne was going through some of Antonio papers and found the registration to his truck. The last name on the registration was different from the last name on there marriage licenses. Antonio wrote to Adrienne after he was taken back to Florida, but she couldn't trust being with him anymore. She gave him the opportunity to tell her the truth before they were married, and he continued to lie to her after she asked him if there was anything he needed to tell her before they were married, and he said no. Adrienne divorced him while he was in prison, he called her once to say that they were going to take away his green card and send him back to Cuba. Then he turned around and called her again saying they had changed their mind about taking his green card. Adrienne never heard from him again after that.

CHAPTER FIVE

Have you ever heard the expression, if it's to good to be true, you better believe something is not right?

Well, Adrienne thought she was being given another chance, and this man was really to good to be true. It was something about him that made her smile from ear to ear every time she saw him. Rick had such a kind and calm spirit about him and that was something Adrienne had never experienced before in a man. Adrienne was praying that he was God sent. She really thought he was an angel sent from heaven just for her. She thought he was the sweetest man you ever wanted to meet, much nicer then any of the other men that crossed her path before him. Everything was fine at first until they made love for the first time. Rick held her and made love to her like no man had ever done before. And it wasn't just sex to her. They waited a long time before making what she thought it was true love for a change. Adrienne wanted to get to know him first. But afterwards guess she didn't wait long enough. Because it wasn't long after they made love that trouble came their way. Adrienne realized they had fallen into sin. They couldn't keep their hands off of one another. Adrienne thought she had found the love of her life, the one man she had been looking for all her life. It was fun at first, going to church together, singing together. Adrienne felt so relieved and free that she had finally met someone who was kind to her for a change. Even though she looked for the good in every one she met. She thought, for sure Rick was the one. The perfect man for her at least, she was hoping he was. Adrienne realized too, Rick was some what sat in his own ways. As was she. But as time went on, she realized that some of Rick's ways were not the way in which she was headed. She just wished she had realized it before she married him. Adrienne was so blinded by love she couldn't see until it was to late. Rick and Adrienne dated for about three years before they got married. They had exchanged promise rings to one another. But no matter what Adrienne was going through she stayed in the word of God everyday seeking wisdom, knowledge and understanding of His word. It helped Adrienne to realize that her ways and her husband Rick ways were not the ways of God. While Adrienne was being sanctified by the word of God she started to take off the old Adrienne and put on the new Adrienne. But her husband Rick became someone she didn't recognize anymore. He wanted to continue to do things his way. Things that were not of God. Adrienne tried to Minister God's word to him, but he didn't want to hear it. Rick wanted to play the piano in the church on Sunday and play R&B music on the side on Saturday night or any other time he could. But Adrienne wanted no part in the R&B music and she told him so. She tried telling Rick he couldn't serve two masters, but he didn't see anything wrong with it. He was hearing from other people that it was nothing wrong with it when his wife was telling him what the Word said. And he still didn't want to hear it. Rick said his pastor told him it was nothing wrong with him playing R&B music because he played the piano also that it was the way people made their living. Adrienne disagreed with Rick, and whom ever it was that told him he could play both gospel and R&B music. God said, we had to love one and hate the other. Adrienne chose to love God. You can't have one foot over here and the other one over there. God said, He would supply all of our needs, and that was what Adrienne believed. Just because other people were doing it doesn't mean you have to too. Rick didn't see anything wrong with doing it. You can't do like everybody else even if you have to stand along. Everyone is responsible for there own soul. Adrienne was striving to be a Christian and not even Rick was going to turn her around from that. The more Adrienne tried to get close to God, the farther the devil took Rick in the opposite direction. Rick could be as arrogant and selfish as he was loving and kind when he wanted to be. He showed that side of himself to Adrienne on more then one occasion. But Adrienne left that between him and God. Adrienne was so much in love with Rick that she thought her love was enough for them both.

It seem the more she loved him the more selfish he became. He turned out to be a wolf in sheep clothing the same way her second husband Walker had been. One was just a little bit more sleek then the other one. It turned out they were both born in the same month which was August. There zodiac sign were Virgo. It was as though Walker her second husband had come they pretended to be one thing on the outside. But there was something totally different was going on, on the inside of them. Adrienne suddenly realized that most people are that way. The Lord knows our hearts, but if you stay around a person long enough, you'll know their heart too. Adrienne thought since Rick was already in the church when they met, that he had God on the inside of him already. But come to fine out the church was not in him. Adrienne thought she should have known better, when his ways wasn't lining up with the word of God. Rick had the zeal of God, but not according to knowledge. Adrienne learned to pray for him, herself, her children, and their children, the way her grandmother prayed for her. So God would be in them and direct their path. But Rick was still determined to do what he wanted too his own way. Although Rick was a very nice man, he always put Adrienne last in every way. She didn't mine him putting God first, but everything and everybody else came before his wife. Rick even put his ex-wife and daughter before Adrienne. They saw more of him then she did and she was his wife. Adrienne read in the Word where Jesus said, husbands love your wives, as God love the church. But Rick was at his ex-wife house everyday like clock work and his wife only saw him three or four days out of the week. Adrienne couldn't get Rick to do any work around the house, he always had an excuse or he didn't have time. But when night came, he was right there to go to bed. Whenever he did show up the two or three nights out of the week he was begging for sex. Adrienne was having problems with her back and neck, but she couldn't even get him to mow the grass. He always made up some kind of excuse to get out of mowing the yard. Adrienne thought she would just love him and let God take care of the rest believing that only God could do the impossible.

James and Adrienne met at church were he was the piano and keyboard player for the choirs. Adrienne was in the adult mass choir. James had been playing piano at the church for over a year or so before they actually had a conversation with one another. Besides, Adrienne was still married to Antonio at the time on paper anyway. Antonio was still in jail for something that happened before Adrienne and he ever met. She was in the process of divorcing him but the divorce wasn't final. She decided to go on with her life without him. Rick and Adrienne got together by accident of cause. They had become friends and interested in one another.

One day some of the church members decided they wanted to purchase a bus for the church. The pastor wanted all of the church members to come out on that Saturday evening before or after choir rehearsal to see what everyone thought of the bus. Before it was to be purchased by the transportation committee. It was a big continental bus nice on the inside and out. Adrienne thought. After rehearsal everyone was on there way out of the church, and Adrienne decided to go and take one more look at the bus as did some of the other members. And there was Rick who just so happen to take a second look at the bus. Rick and Adrienne started up a conversation about how nice the bus was. And their conversation continued from there by him asking her what her relationship was to the elderly woman he sometime played the music for when she sung in the church. The woman he was talking about was Adrienne's grandmother on her dad's side of the family. Adrienne's grandmother loved to give God Praise. And Adrienne loved listening to her grandmother sing. But some of the people in the church didn't like her singing every Sunday. So they went to the pastor wanting him to stop her from singing. The pastor had the nerve to ask Adrienne to ask her grandmother not to sing in church unless she was asked to sing. That hurt Adrienne to have to go to her grandmother and tell her they didn't want her singing in the church anymore unless she was asked to sing. Adrienne didn't know if they were jealous of her grandmother singing or what the deal was. But her grandmother keep right on singing God's praises. God rest her soul, Adrienne's grandmother lived less then two months of being One hundred and five years old. Rick said to Adrienne that he use to play for her grandmother when she would sing at another church were Adrienne's uncle was the pastor. As they continued talking, come to find out Rick already knew most of Adrienne's family members. But Adrienne he didn't know. Adrienne didn't go all that much to other churches the way Rick did. By him being a piano player he got to go to a lot of different churches with the choirs he played for. It wasn't until Adrienne rededicated her life to Christ that she joined and started singing with the choir. Which was a year or two before Rick became the new piano player. Adrienne gave her life to Christ at the age of six. She didn't understand what it all about at that age. But felt she needed to be baptized. The water was deep and cold. Adrienne was baptized in a pond behind the church. She was so afraid of the water because she knew she couldn't swim. But only God knew what was in the water. He kept her through it all. Rick and Adrienne stood outside of the church and talked for a long time that night. It had gotten real late by the time they realized just how late it was. They said their good-byes and went their separate ways. Every Sunday after that it seemed, Rick would come up to Adrienne with a question about something. Rick and Adrienne's daughter Ariel were friends already. By Ariel singing in the youth and adult choir and a long time band member through out high school. She and Rick were already connected through music. Rick too was a long time band member in college. So they had music in common already. Adrienne thought about, one Sunday the church was having dinner. She and Rick sat just across the table from each other eating and they never said a word to each other. It wasn't until after they had finished eating that she ran into Rick and her daughter Ariel talking in the hallway of the church leading to the door. Rick had left the table before Adrienne. Adrienne's daughter Ariel introduced them to one another. Rick said to Adrienne that whenever he forgot the tune to a song he would ask Ariel and she would sound it out for him. All the time Rick had been playing piano for the church, he never knew Adrienne was Ariel mother until that day. Adrienne didn't hang around much after church. She would speak to people on her way out the door and she went home to rest. Adrienne knew people thought she was stuck up. But she was trying to show no emotion to the pain, because she didn't want people to know just how bad she was hurting. Adrienne had no idea herself what was going on. She was really stressed feeling like she had the weight of the world on her shoulders. Like the woman with the issue of blood, Adrienne went from doctor to doctor spending all of her money until she had no more money to spend. Depression set in. Adrienne was so tied of people treating her as though she was crazy. But still she pressed her way to get to church on Sunday morning, even when she didn't feel like getting out of bed. She asked the Lord for strength to keep moving.

On those days when Adrienne really felt bad she would stay at home. She tried to hide what she was going through from her children. Adrienne felt she was to young to be feeling the way she felt. The medications she took had her walking around like a zombie most of the time. She was in her early forties and felt like she was trapped inside of a ninety something year old body. The pain was so intense at times. She started to fall down sometime for no reason. It took her falling down for the fourth times before she realized something was really wrong and it had to been coming from the medication she was taking. After receiving a print out of her medications. Sure enough that was the problem, the print out said, off bounce and clumsy. That just added to the pain Adrienne was already in. She sprung her ankle in one of the falls. And as time when on she got to where she could hardly walk without using a stick to help her. After all of that, man still refused to put her back on disability. She was catching hell trying to get back on it. Every time she was denied she had it appealed.

As time passed Adrienne noticed Rick would come to church one Sunday with curls, and the next Sunday without curls in his hair. So she thought would ask him if she could style his hair the next time it needed fixing just to see what was going on with his hair. But later on she realized that it wasn't the person fixing his hair that wasn't during a good job, but it was Rick using the wrong product on his hair that took out his curls. He didn't know how to maintain it himself. The Lord had blessed Adrienne to be able to attend college the way she always wanted to do. Where she graduated top of her class with honors while receiving her cosmetology licenses. It was tough but she asked God to help her each and ever day inspire of the pain. While in college, Adrienne made up in her mind she wanted to open her very own beauty salon. She thought that way she could work at her own pace and that would help her pain. But it didn't work out that way. After working at a fast pace for so many years her body had slowed down with pain all over as though it couldn't go anymore. She didn't have the strength or energy to do the little things. But she continued to ask God to help her a lone the way.

One Sunday after church services were over, the choir had been invited to another church for their choir day program. And just before the program started at the church Rick walked up to where Adrienne was sitting and out of the blue he asked her where she lived. And she applied to him that it was just around the corner from the church where they were. Adrienne didn't think anything about him asking her where she lived at the time. She was hoping the program wouldn't go on too long so she could go home and lay down from having to set so long. She thought it was strange that he would come up to her wanting to know where she lived. After the choir finished with their two songs, Adrienne decided she would go on home. She left just before the program was about to be over. After being in church all day starting with Sunday school then worship service then on to another church. Adrienne was tied. She tried to support the church and choir as much as she could in spite of the pain. She was feeling pretty stiff, tied and sore all over, which was the way she felt mostly every day. But she kept pressing her way to be at church on Sunday, Wednesday night bible class, and Saturday night choir rehearsal. Nothing else mattered. She had time to rest on the days in between so she would have the energy to keep going. Adrienne was diagnosed with fibromyalgia, and rheumatoid arthritis, the same as her grandmother.

The following Sunday Adrienne and her daughter were on their way home from church. Adrienne let her daughter Ariel do the driving. Adrienne looked up just in time to see that it was Rick driving in front of them. As they moved over into the turning lane to go home Adrienne blew the horn at Rick as they both had to stop at the stop sign in front of them. As they drove right up beside Rick to the left as he was going to keep straight. Adrienne yelled out the window telling him that this was the way in which she lived. Rick turned in behind them and followed them home. There was going to be a youth program at the church later on that evening, Adrienne later learned that Rick decided not to go all the way back home since he lived a distance away. He was on his way to get a bite to eat and visit with a friend he knew in the area. But his plans were changed as he ended up at Adrienne's house instead. Adrienne invited Rick to eat with them since she had cooked the night before. All she had to do was warm the food in the microwave. While they were eating, Adrienne struck up a conversation about Rick's hair. She was looking for some new claimants anyway so she ask Rick if maybe she could fix his hair the next time he needed for it to be done, he said yes. It had gotten close to time to head back out to the church. But Adrienne didn't have the energy to go back after being in church through Sunday school and worship service. She asked Rick if he wouldn't mind taking Ariel back to the program with him. She just needed to rest for a little while. The medication she was taking made her very sleepy. Something very strange was going on with her body that she didn't quit understand what was going on. She would get very tied all of a sudden as though she didn't have the energy to go anymore. She asked Ariel, if she would go back to the church with Rick. To show him the way back to the highway leading to the church and Adrienne said, she would pick her up from the church by the time she thought the program was over, which usually took about two hours. Adrienne said, she wouldn't recommend any parent to let their child go anywhere with anybody they didn't know. It is not safe. There are some twisted people in the world. It is hard to trust Christians and even harder to trust those that are not. The word tells us to trust no man. Men tend to think with that little head in between their legs instead of that big head on their shoulders. But Adrienne knew the youth were going to march in the church at the beginning of the program and Rick had to be at the church on time in order for them to march in. Adrienne just needed to lay down and take a nap before driving. By the time she got to the church, people were getting in their cars to leave. Adrienne got out of her car just in time enough to see Rick driving out of the parking lot, as he wave to her saying he would see them the following weekend at rehearsal. Saturday came and Adrienne had a song she wanted to try and sing with the choir. But she was always nervous about singing in front of people. She could carry a really good tune at home. But when it came to singing in front of people, Lord help her, her nerves kicked in causing her voice to crack. She had tried to sing that same song once before. Before Rick became the church piano player. Adrienne decided she wanted to try and sing it again. But her voice still cracked. Rick refused to let her give up trying to sing. Adrienne thought, that was nice of Rick to help her. Adrienne decided she want to go and take voice lessons at the college where she had graduated from earlier. Hoping to get over her fear of having to sing in front of people. At the same time Rick still wouldn't let her give up trying. That was what Adrienne liked about him, he always tried to help others when it came to singing. He would call Adrienne up to sing a song that they had practiced on together at his house or her'. And little did the other choir members know. Rick was helping her to overcome her fear of singing in front of people. He was helping her with her voice assignments as well. Adrienne could tell some of the other choir members were jealous. They started to get very jealous of the fact that Rick would call Adrienne up to sing. She was trying her best to praise God for blessing her to finally be able to go to college. She wanted to praise God in song for what He was doing in her life, and for what He had already brought her through. She believed in her heart, God had given her a second chance to get it right. God had blessed her to go back and get her high school diploma, and then He blessed her to be able to go on to college. It was a few years later. But she made it. Adrienne wanted more and better out of life. But the devil had to show his ugly face trying to stop her from getting to where God wanted her to be. Adrienne started college at the same time her oldest daughter Audrey did. Rick would help her with the music part of her voice lesson assignments so much to the point that it inspired her to write a song, and then another song. Rick produced the songs and from there they went on with the help of the Lord to form a gospel group. Adrienne was so nervous but happy to be singing, everything was happening so fast. She just wanted to praise the Lord even more. "The Praise Team "was the name she had come up with for the group. But as time went on, she could see and feel that they were being treated differently by those who she thought were her church family and friends. Jealousy showed it's ugly face and Adrienne got discouraged. But kept going. At first she thought it was the name of the group people didn't like, so with God's help they voted and decided to change the name of the group to "The Praise Believers" instead. That didn't make things any better. The devil got even busy, and people started saying and doing stupid stuff right to there faces. But they kept right on singing.

It wasn't long before Adrienne discovered Rick was smoking marijuana. She went to his house one night. She needed for him to put the music to a song on tape for her. She had to sing the song before the class the next day, so she asked Rick if he wouldn't mind putting the music to the song on tape, so she could practice on it at home. Well, as he was in the middle of playing and recording the music, their came a knock at the door. Rick went to see whom it was. The voice at the door asked if they could speak to Rick outside. While Adrienne was sitting waiting for his return she just so happen to look down at the floor. To make sure her eyes wasn't playing tricks on her she reached down and picked it up. And sure enough, it was a piece of a joint. She started to get her tape and leave, but she wasn't one to over react. When Rick came back in side the house Adrienne asked him if he smoked marijuana. Rick said, he did. Adrienne wanted to walk away right then, but she couldn't something wouldn't let her. Adrienne had fallen in love with Rick already, and she didn't want to lose what they had going together. Rick had been hiding it from her, but now that she knew, he didn't try hiding it anymore. Some how Adrienne ended up smoking it with him, and lost herself in what he was doing. For five years Adrienne smoked off and on with Rick, he was her supplier. Things were good for a while then they started to go down hill. As long as Rick could keep Adrienne high, he got to do whatever he wanted. The moment Adrienne asked the Lord to deliver her from smoking marijuana, Rick got crazy and decided he didn't have to take care of his wife anymore.

The first time they sang together as a group was so amazing to Adrienne that the Lord had blessed her to come out of that shell she was in. She felt so good inside for the first time in her life since her mother passed away. But at the same time the devil saw something good happening and tried very hard to put a stop to it. Rick said to Adrienne from the start that people were going to act a fool. She didn't know what he was talking about at first. But the moment the choir members found out they were dating all hell broke loose and sure enough they did just that, act a fool. Adrienne hadn't experienced how envious, jealous, hateful and backbiting church folk could be until she begin working for the Lord. All those things the Lord said for man not to be. Adrienne thought just because she minded her own business other people would do the same. But she was wrong to even think that way. Adrienne started to experience all the stares at her when she walked into the church. She felt very uncomfortable each Sunday, Wednesday night bible study and choir rehearsal. Some of Adrienne's own relatives turned against her. Adrienne thought church was the last place people would act a fool. But she was wrong again. She thought her life was going to get better after she gave her life to Christ. But little did she know. The devil got just that much more busy seeking to destroy her. The devil had another trap for her and she fell right into it. She realized the more she strive to do good, and service God, the more angry the devil got trying to stop her from praising God. Adrienne asked God to deliver her from smoking cigarettes, and marijuana, and He did. It wasn't until later that she realized that because she followed after temptation, by smoking marijuana, and having sex outside of marriage. Things turned for the worse because of her disobedience to God. After asking God to deliver her from marijuana she tried to smoke once again and couldn't. The smoke burned her throat so she had no chose but to quit. She ended up having to quit her job because of the constant pain she was in. She had a doctor to turn her down for medical care. The doctor said, it was because she didn't have time for the paper work. Adrienne needed her disability restored. She had experienced a spasm on her left side and didn't have money to go to the doctor and at the time she didn't know she could have gone to the emergency room. She couldn't get anybody to help her. Adrienne called on the name of Jesus to help her and He came to her rescue. Adrienne had to close down her business, because she couldn't afford to keep it opened. She worked hard to make a success of her business, she even tried working in spite of the pain, but it didn't last. Some people wanted Adrienne to do their hair, but wasn't willing to pay for her services. Or they wanted to get their hair done one day and claim they would come back and pay her another day, and they never came back. Adrienne thought, the more she try to help people, they let her down. Adrienne was already in pain, the more she tried the worse her pain became. Her husband Rick turned his back on her when she needed him the most. He thought in his mind she didn't want to work. She forgave him so she could go on and do what she had to do to take care of herself with the help of the Lord. To Rick, it was more important for him to take care of his grown daughter, the ex-wife, grandchildren and his mama, then it was for him to take care of his wife. She believe Rick was being influenced by them along with the weed he was smoking to keep him from doing what he was suppose to as her husband. But Adrienne thanked God for keeping her in her right mind when she thought she was going to lose her mind. The thought of her flesh and blood kin turning on her, was more then she could bear alone. But she heard her pastor preach, that it may hurt, but it want work. Adrienne gave it over to God. She had given her life over to Christ at the age of six years old. She really didn't understand what it was all about at that age, but she was glad she did, because she knew it was God that kept her through it all. Adrienne realized that if she hadn't given her life over to Christ, only God knows were she would be today. The devil tried so many times to kill her. She became a born again, baptized Holy Ghost filled believer in Christ Jesus. It was January twenty fourth nineteen ninety—four on a Monday that Adrienne was born again. She made it a habit to repent everyday for her sins as she studied the Bible everyday for God to sanctify her soul.

It all started one Saturday night after choir rehearsal that Rick made his way over to Adrienne's house for her to do his hair. Since some one had already relaxed Rick hair with chemicals a couple of weeks before, Adrienne decided she would just style his hair. He offered to pay her, but she wouldn't except his money. Adrienne told him, she just wanted to see what was going on with his hair. She explained to him that some time he had curls in his hair and sometime he didn't. Adrienne asked him some questions concerning his hair. Like what kind of products he used on his hair? And after he told her, she realized he was using the wrong product on his hair. She told him the right product to use. After that Rick left, telling Adrienne and her daughter Ariel he would see them the next day at church. Sunday morning comes, and as Adrienne walked from where she had been teaching her kindergarten Sunday school class. All of a sudden, she heard her daughter Ariel, laugh out loud. She could tell her child's voice anywhere. As she turned to look at her, Ariel pointed out the fact that Rick and Adrienne were wearing the same color clothing, which was royal blue. Adrienne smiled and continued on into the sanctuary of the church. Adrienne took that to be a sign from God that this man was her husband. After church was over, Rick asked Adrienne if he could take her to dinner for doing his hair since she wouldn't take any money from him. Adrienne graciously excepted the invitation. While on their way to the restaurant, Rick accidentally ran over something that was lying in the highway. He tried to dodge whatever it was. But Rick managed to run it over anyway. Adrienne thought, Rick was as nervous as she was since she hadn't been on a date or eaten out in a long time. What neither one of them knew at the time was whatever Rick hit on the highway, put a hole in one of his tires causing a slow leak. It wasn't until they walked out of the restaurant that they noticed the tire was on flat. They only had like thirty minutes or so to get to the church where they had been invited for their choir day program. Rick drove to a service station to air up the tire, but the air was coming back out as fast as he put it in. A deacon from the church stopped by to see if Rick needed some help. But Rick was going to need a new tire. Adrienne asked, the deacon if he wouldn't mine taking them to her house to get her car, seeing that they only had a few minutes to get to the church. Adrienne needed to pickup her daughter Ariel from the house anyway. The tire had to wait till they got back. They were a little bit late getting to the church. The program had just started, and what do you know? The devil was waiting when they got there. When it came time for the choir to sing, the person that was suppose to lead the first song decided she didn't want to sing the song the choir had rehearsed on the night before. But what she wanted was to show off with another sung in front of her co-workers, the way she usually did when the choir had to go somewhere. The woman must have forgotten that it wasn't about her pleasing her friends, but it was all about pleasing God for Him to get the glory. Rick started playing the music to the song they had rehearsed on the night before. The woman stood there in front of all those people and wouldn't sing. She said to Rick, she was not going to sing that song. Instead of her going over to him before he started playing to let him know, it was requested that she sing another song. The woman just stood there, Rick didn't know why she wouldn't sing, so he just stopped playing. Then the woman started singing another song. After that it was time for the second song to be sung, and what do you know, the devil wasn't finished yet, the next person that was to lead the next song got up and did the exact same thing as the first person. She too decided she wanted to sing another song instead of the one that was rehearsed the night before. What Rick and Adrienne didn't realize was the deacon had gotten to the church before them. It was too much hatred, jealousy, and envy going on in the choir, and Adrienne could see it and she wanted no part in it. Adrienne did what she was asked to do and sat down. It never occurred to the two of them what was going on. But later on they realized that some of the members of the church was acting cold toward them as though they hated seeing the two of them together. That Sunday was the first time any of the choir members had seen the two of them together and that was when the members started acting crazy toward them. They were being picked on, and lied on, but they never said a word. Rick tried to warn Adrienne it was going to be that way once the members found out they were dating. But Adrienne thought since she minded her own business, other people should mine theirs. Which they should, but it didn't turn out that way. The devil saw something good happening and he wanted to put a stop to it. From that day on some of the choir members made it their business to keep confusion going on in the choir. All Adrienne was thinking about was praising the Lord Jesus Christ in song. Some of the choir members got so jealous of Adrienne because she and Rick were practicing and singing new songs together, and that really made the devil mad. When the devil saw he couldn't stop Rick and Adrienne, they lied on them to the pastor, and they were sitting stumbling blocks in their way. One woman was so mad at Rick and Adrienne she went to the pastor and told him that they were arguing in the church. Adrienne wondered why this woman would be sitting in church looking at what a husband and wife do in the first place. What business was it of hers what they were doing? But all Rick and Adrienne were doing was trying to figure out what songs the youth were going to sing that day. Adrienne asked Rick if he would go out to the truck and get her briefcase so they could see what two songs the youth were going to sing. The woman was mad because at one time she was the youth director, and for some reason she decided to go and sit down and not direct the youth. And Rick asked Adrienne if she would direct the youth that Saturday doing rehearsal. Once Adrienne started directing the youth, the woman didn't like that at all. The youth were sounding better and on key, and that devil couldn't stand that. The time came for the youth to vote for a youth director. No one bothered to tell Adrienne they were going to be voting for youth director until she got to the church for what she thought was rehearsal. This woman and her two sisters had everything already planned out what they were going to do. And that did not enclosed Adrienne. Most of the youth was the woman's children and her sister's children, so it was easy for them to turn the youth against Adrienne. They had already decided what they were going to do before Adrienne ever got there. It was all a setup. The woman's sister joined the church a few weeks or so before all of this went down. Evidently the sisters had gotten together and called all of Adrienne's family members that were in the youth choir and told them there was not going to be a choir rehearsal that day because none of Adrienne's family members showed up for rehearsal that day. Only the woman's children and her sister's children were there. And they voted for the woman's sister to be the youth director even though she knew less about directing then her sister. Their plan didn't work the way they thought because once the pastor watched this woman's sister direct. He asked Adrienne if she would be the assistant director. Adrienne would direct one youth Sunday and the woman's sister directed the next youth Sunday. Adrienne could tell the sister was catching on to the way she was directing and she got better at it. This woman managed to turned all the youth against Adrienne, she could tell when some of the youth started giving her the cold shoulder by not wanting to sing when Adrienne directed. They did everything they could to make Adrienne look bad in front of the pastor. When the devil couldn't stop Adrienne from doing what she do, that made the devil madder. The bad part about it all was, the pastor sided with the ones that was keeping up all the hell in the church, as if they had nothing better to do then to try and make Adrienne look bad. Adrienne was always shy, quiet and never had much to say, and they used that to there advantage taking Adrienne's kindness for weakness. The women married, unmarried and the woman on the organ, she went out of her way to get under Adrienne's skin. She thought Adrienne was going to act a fool in the church like her. But that would have made Adrienne no better then her, the woman got in the habit of walking up to Rick after church. But as soon as Adrienne walked up, she stop talking as though she had something to hide or to make Adrienne think their was something going on between the two of them. The woman would say and do stuff kind of on a sly. But Adrienne paid the woman no mine as she held her peace. Adrienne finally realized the woman wanted Rick for herself. But her plan backfired. Rick said, he wasn't interested in the woman. But was trying to help her play the right coils to the music. Rick said, to Adrienne that one of the guys at the church. The woman's brother said, to him that a few of the women in the church had a crush on him. Rick said, to Adrienne that the only thing he was interested in was playing the music right and going home. That was all Adrienne needed to hear. But that still didn't stop the woman from getting in Rick's face every chance she got. Until one day as the choir was getting on the bus to travel to another church out of town. Rick and Adrienne would always sit two or three seats back at the front of the bus. This particular day Adrienne got on the bus and set on the third row of seats near the window, leaving the isle seat open for Rick to get on the bus. And the woman decided she would sat on the opposite side of Adrienne and Rick on the second row of seats. The woman turned around in her seat to carry on a conversation with Rick while Adrienne was on the phone with one of her daughters. From the end of the conversation Adrienne had with her daughter, Rick could tell Adrienne was upset as she got off the phone. Rick took Adrienne by the hand holding it in his as he reclined his seat and closed his eyes to sleep doing the trip. Traveling back home, the woman decided not to ride the bus back home. She was mad that Rick didn't have to say a word. But showed her that he and Adrienne were together. Rick thought everybody was just being friendly to him. But really that is how the devil works. Rick was very nigh eve to the fact that everybody wasn't his friend. People will stab you in the back and look you in the face at the same time. Rick would just take it with a smile and went on about his business. Adrienne thought Rick was a chicken by him letting people talk to him any kind of way. But

God did say for us to stand still and He would fight our battles for us. Rick was sometime over friendly, Adrienne thought. Rick said, he was the same way with everybody. But Adrienne thought he was more over friendly with the women. He was somewhat of a player. Rick would sometime say things to other women he never said to her. Like hello darling, they were older women he knew. But still Adrienne thought that was being disrespectful to her. Adrienne tried several times to break things off with Rick because she was being treated really bad right in church, by people she never had a problem with before she got involved with him. Adrienne was hated and envied by people for no reason. Adrienne thought it had to be because the two of them were going places and singing together in other churches. Adrienne felt very uncomfortable and nervous, but they kept right on praising God. The more Adrienne tried to keep her mind stayed on Jesus. The more the devil attacked her through those that claim to love the Lord. Adrienne had gotten hooked on Rick thinking the Lord was on the inside of him. Rick and Adrienne had one thing in common, and that was their love for music, singing and a good heart when it came to other people. A heart filled with love to give. God said, He would make your enemies your footstool, and vengeance was His. And that is what Adrienne believed. The fact that she believed in God's word she was hated even more. Rick made Adrienne laugh more than any man had before him and that helped take away some of the sadness for a while. The more they praised the Lord together, the worse the devil became in their lives. Adrienne knew, as long as she had God on her side she could keep striving to make it home in heaven. God said, in His word that many are the afflictions of the righteous, but God will deliver us out of them all. And that's what Adrienne believed.

God blessed Rick and Adrienne to have a gospel group. The devil really got busy. They were writing and singing their own songs. They one day decided to go to the studio where Rick's brother had a part time business on the side to record the songs. They should have never let anyone know what they were doing because they found out very quickly, not everyone is for you. Some of the people in the church had good paying jobs, so did Adrienne at one time. But the people that paid big money in the church were the ones that got to make all the decisions concerning the church. Adrienne paid her tides when she had it to pay once she came to the knowledge that that was what she was suppose to do. Even though sometime she didn't have a job and not having a job mean not having any money. The church folk just kept something going all the time instead of concentrating on what the word of God said. To Adrienne, she couldn't speak for Rick, but to her it was all about getting to know the Lord for herself. For all the trails and tribulations He had brought her through. Adrienne was being persecuted for God's sake because of the gifts God had given her.

As Rick and Adrienne were about to get married, Adrienne decided she was going to get her blood test after she had finished up with a claimant that day. She stepped inside the house to get ready, then she went back out into the salon to get something she had left there. Adrienne made the mistake of laying down her keys while she straightened up a little before walking out and locking the door behind her leaving her keys inside the salon. She had a second set of keys, but they were in the house hanging on the wall. Adrienne had to find a way to get in the house to get the other set of keys. It wasn't easy, everything was locked down tight. Adrienne couldn't even get back into the salon. Once Adrienne found a way into the house, she went on and had the blood test.

After three years of dating, Adrienne and Rick finally got married. Adrienne had to push Rick into getting married, which she realized later on was a big mistake. She thought, they had lived in sin long enough. Adrienne had to cut off the sex in order for him to say I do. And the hell people were putting them through, even getting married didn't stop the devils from coming after them. Things got just that much worse after they got married. One morning Adrienne and Rick were on their way into the church for Sunday school. Adrienne heard this woman say, hey good looking. She either didn't see Adrienne, or she said it for the hell of it because Adrienne was there with Rick. At first Adrienne was walking behind Rick, he was a little taller then she was and he walked faster too. This woman was dropping her mother off at the church. She helped her mother up the steps and when she looked up again, Adrienne was walking beside Rick. Adrienne didn't say a word, she just acted like she didn't even hear the woman, so did Rick. The woman got back in her car and left the church. Adrienne thought she must have been too embarrassed to stay for church, or she had to work instead of staying for church. Adrienne said she bet the woman mouth could have dropped to the ground when she looked up and saw her walking beside Rick long as her mouth was. The woman couldn't look Adrienne in the face after that. Adrienne knew what she was all about, and tried not to let that bother her. Adrienne thought she would let God continue to fight her battles as He had so many times before. The woman probably had been flirting with him all the time when Adrienne wasn't with him. Rick never said a word about it, but Adrienne knew he was bad about flirting with women right in her face so it was no telling what he was doing behind her back.

Rick's daughter Niece, from his first marriage was another battle Adrienne needed God to fight for her. Niece was contently in between Adrienne and Rick in some way or another. Rick put her there by spoiling her and therefore always put her before Adrienne. Adrienne thought, maybe it was because Niece was Rick only child. Rick was protective of her as she was graduating high school. From the looks of it Rick was protective of her all of her life. Niece acted as though she didn't have a life of her own. She had to be wherever Rick was. When Niece was away from Rick she would call him what seem like every thirty minutes to see where he was. Or either he would call Niece every thirty minutes if he hadn't heard from her in that length of time. Adrienne tried to talk to Rick about it but he couldn't see it. Rick chose to spend more time with Niece then he did with Adrienne. Adrienne was blinded by love and she thought things would change after they got married but they didn't. Neither one of them could turn around without knowing where the other one was. Niece was living with her mother but she was at Rick house everyday. If she wasn't there she would call him or he was calling her three, four, five times a day to see what the other one was doing. Adrienne thought, maybe she wouldn't have a problem with it if Niece had been a small child. But she was about to graduate high school. This was something new to Adrienne. She never knew two people to be so close. They were to close Adrienne thought for a father and daughter. Adrienne realized she never got any attention at all like that from her dad. He was to busy working and never had time to show her that kind of love. She never even heard her daddy tell her he loved her because he wasn't there when she needed him. After Niece graduated from high school she signed up for the air force. She was only going to be gone six weeks for basic training. She called Rick every time you looked around crying she wanted to come home. Adrienne stopped over Rick house one evening. The phone rang constantly the whole time she was there. It was Niece crying to Rick that she wanted to come home. Rick said, he was trying to encourage her to stay there until her time was up. But all Adrienne could see was that Rick had spoiled her, enabling her, the same way her second husband had done there daughter Ariel, spoil her. Adrienne just traded in one kind of abuser for another kind of abuser. It was something all the time with Niece. When it came time for Niece to graduate from basic training for some reason, Rick didn't want Adrienne to go with him to the graduation. He didn't even want her to take him to the airport. Adrienne thought that to be strange. But she figured, maybe his ex-wife was going with him. And he didn't want her to know. Rick claim she didn't go but Adrienne had known him to lie to lie her before. When Rick and Adrienne first started dating, he told her he wasn't dating anyone. But one night as they were sitting watching television at Rick house. Their came a knock at the door, some woman wanted to talk to Rick outside. Rick hadn't long got out of the shower so he didn't have on a shirt. He goes outside with no shirt on leaving Adrienne in the house alone. After a while Adrienne goes to the door to see what was taking Rick so long to come back inside. As she opened the door she didn't see Rick but their was a little boy out side playing around. Adrienne asked the little boy where Rick was? The little boy said they were around the house. Adrienne thought to herself, why would they be around the house? Adrienne closed the door wondering what was so important that they had to go around the house and talk. She remembered he wasn't wearing a shirt when he left out the door. She looked around and there was a shirt on the back of the couch. She went back and opened the door calling out to the little boy to take the shirt to Rick but he came from around the house. Adrienne gave him the shirt, and as he put it on. The woman he had been talking to came out from around the house. Adrienne asked, the woman who she was? And she said she and Rick were dating. Rick said to Adrienne that he was her mentor. He was trying to help her get her GED. Then the woman showed Adrienne a ring that Rick had given her. But it was the same ring Adrienne had given Rick a couple of weeks before. Rick claim the woman took the ring off his finger and wouldn't give it back to him. Adrienne said to the woman that she had given Rick the ring and she wanted it back. The woman said she got the ring from Rick so she gave the ring back to him. As soon as the woman gave Rick back the ring

Adrienne asked him to give it back to her. The woman asked Rick for the gold chain back he had around his neck. He took it off and gave it to her. Then she decided to give it back to him and he took it and put it back around his neck. Adrienne knew then that there was more going on then Rick said. Adrienne decided she was going to leave because he had lied to her about not dating anyone when they meet. Rick wanted his cake and eat it too. But got caught. Adrienne gathered all the stuff she had given Rick and left. She rolled and smoked a joint while she was setting in the car. As she had time to calm down, she thought to herself she wasn't going to let the devil win this time. After the woman left, Adrienne went back to the house to asked Rick why if nothing was going on between him and the woman why did he take the chain back from her? Rick said, because she gave it to him. That to Adrienne was the wrong answer! She pulled the chain from Rick's neck breaking it into pieces. Adrienne said to Rick, he was not going to make a fool of her, not again. He was not going to be wearing some other woman chain around his neck not while he was with her. Now that Adrienne thought about it, it wasn't the devil trying to keep them apart. But it was God showing her who Rick really was. The first time was when she found out he was smoking marijuana, the second time was when this woman showed up at his house saying they were dating. The third time was when Adrienne locked her keys in the salon. Strike three your out. Adrienne ignored all the warning signs. She had fallen in love with Rick because she thought he had such a kind heart and he made her laugh. She realized too late that it was all a trick of the enemy. It was the marijuana Rick was smoking that tricked Adrienne into thinking he was a kind person. It had to be the marijuana she was smoking that made her think that just because Rick was in the church he was saved. He was pretending to be saved the way most people do. It was a shock to Adrienne when she looked at the way other people acted in the church. It hurt her to her heart something terrible because it was no different then smoking marijuana and being in the church. Adrienne realized she was hurting herself though and not other people. She forgave Rick that night as they made love and the tears rolled from Adrienne's eyes. There was another time Rick lied to her. It was a holiday coming up and Rick said, to Adrienne he had to work that day. So Adrienne thought she would surprise him by going over to his house and prepare dinner for him when he got home. But when she got to the house, the surprise was on her. Rick was there and so was his daughter Niece. He didn't have to work at all. He was still in his pajamas that Adrienne had brought for him. That told her that he didn't have to work. Adrienne asked Rick, why he lied to her about having to work and he didn't? Rick said, to Adrienne he wanted to spend the day with his daughter. When Adrienne asked him, why he didn't just tell her that? Rick said, he didn't know how to tell her because he didn't know how she would take it. Adrienne looked at their relationship and thought about the relationship she never had with her dad. And they lived in the same house. Adrienne didn't have a close relationship with her dad before or after her mother passed. She didn't know her dad was her dad until she was well into her teen years. Rick and Niece relationship was strange to Adrienne for a father and daughter. Adrienne felt that lying seem to come natural to Rick. Adrienne caught Rick once again in that same lie. Once Niece returned home from basic training she decided not to go back in the air force. But decide she would go to college instead. Rick helped her move her stuff on campus at the college. Adrienne was surprised when Rick invited her to go along with them since the college was less than an hour drive from where he lived. Niece couldn't even stay on campus, she wined about every little thing. Even though she was suppose to be living on campus, she would drive home every night putting more miles on the car then needed to be. Rick said to Adrienne that he wanted to support Niece until she was twenty-five years old. Adrienne didn't like the fact that Rick was enabling Niece, but that was his child so she tried not to interfere with the two of them. Because Adrienne didn't interfere things went from bad to worse. Rick continued taking care of Niece well into her thirties and her four children. Adrienne only found out about it a few weeks before Rick passed away. He was taking care of this ex-wife as well. Rick said, to Adrienne one day that she should be able to take care of herself. Adrienne believe Niece along with her mother was poisoning Rick's mind against her, because Rick went from giving her fifty to seventy-five dollars a week to help her pay her bills, to nothing at all. Adrienne decided she would do just that with the help of the Lord, her daughter Audrey and her son-in –law. Adrienne thanked God and them for having her back. Niece was now in her thirties with four children. Rick went from taking care of Niece and her mother to taking care of his mother and his four grandchildren and that didn't leave any room for him to take care of Adrienne because he stopped doing anything for her. Rick forgot he had a wife. Everything was all about him and what he wanted to do. He was never there for Adrienne when she needed for him to be. He put everything and everybody before her. Adrienne was the last thing he thought about and that was at the end of the day. When he wanted to have sex, then he'd come knocking at her door. She treated him as her husband every time he showed up at the door. Rick thought Adrienne should have had her own money while he was supporting his daughter. Adrienne would of had her own money had it not been for her condition. Rick thought Adrienne was being lazy and didn't want to work. But she was experiencing pain all over her body.

She tried to work. With Rick stressing her on top of what she was already going through, didn't help.

Rick only made the situation worse, by not doing what he was suppose to as her husband. God said, in His word for husbands to love their wives as God love the church. Like the woman at the well, Adrienne had five husbands whom she choose, but they were not the husbands God choose for her. Adrienne did her best to support herself when she opened her own business, with no help from Rick. She thought she would be able to work at her own pace after working at a fast pace all those years. She even walked some days picking up cans beside the road. Even that was painful, but Adrienne knew she had to do something. She asked God to give her strength with every step. Rick knew Adrienne didn't have any income coming in the house. He was stingy with his money.

Niece decided she didn't like the college she was attending, and wanted to attend another college in the same town. Adrienne couldn't understand why Niece didn't get a job and work while she was going to college the way she did. The way her daughter Audrey did. And the way she had seen other people do. That would have taken some of the load off of Rick but he continued to enable her instead of teaching her in the way she should go, and she was willing to let him spoil her. Rick wasn't considerate of Adrienne's feelings at all. Adrienne didn't mine Rick helping Niece out financially as long as she was in college. But to Adrienne, it seemed like Niece didn't want Rick with her. Niece was always right there with her hand out for Rick to give her some money. As long as he gave her money ever time she asked, she was never going to get a job. And she didn't work, even after she started having children.

Rick then took care of her and baby. Niece was never going to get a job as long as Rick was giving her money. Adrienne had a feeling Niece's mother was putting her up to getting every penny she could from Rick. So he wouldn't give Adrienne any money. For the last years of Adrienne and Rick's marriage, Rick didn't suppose Adrienne financially at all. She suffered without because he went a different direct of where God told him to go. He turned out to be someone Adrienne didn't recognize anymore.

Rick said, to Adrienne one day he was about to lose his house, both car, and truck. Rick's eyes had gotten bigger then his wallet. Adrienne tried to warn him, but he want people to think he was more then what he really was. Rick managed to get his house back. He didn't bother to tell Adrienne how he managed to keep the house. Adrienne found out by accident from his mother. Adrienne asked Rick when was he going to tell her he had gotten his house back? He said, to Adrienne he wasn't going to tell her. Rick very much needed to get his priorities straight. That was the reason why they didn't living together in the same house, because he never acted like a husband. He thought he could get married and still do what he wanted. He continued taking care of Niece by letting her move into his house. While he was paying the bills, she kept having babies, even after she had graduated college. Rick moved in the house with his mother instead of moving in with his wife. He said, to Adrienne that his mother had gotten up in age and someone needed to be there with her. Adrienne never could understand why he had to move in with his mother and his sister moved in their dad. But he wanted to sleep with Adrienne in her bed whenever it was convenient for him. Adrienne learned just before Rick passed away the reason he didn't tell her he had gotten his house back was because he had filed bankruptcy on his house along with his ex-wife house as though they were still married. Adrienne just so happen to find the court papers in the truck when Rick asked her to go into the truck to get some papers he knew she was going to need after he found out he had cancer. According to the date on the papers, Adrienne and Rick were married when those papers were filed. Rick began trying to put things in order once he learned he had cancer. He was having complications and had to go into the hospital. He called Adrienne to come to the hospital and be with him. Striving to be a better Christian she goes to the hospital to be at his side. She waited on him hand and foot. But the more she did for him, the more he wanted her to do. Not considering the fact that she was having problems herself, but she was doing what she could for him out of the goodness of her heart. Everyday he was in the hospital Adrienne was praying that God would heal him. Adrienne read all the books she could, on the type of cancer he had. So she would know what to expect from the side effects of his treatment. She was at the hospital with him for eighteen straight days only leaving his side to go to the chapel to pray for him. A couple of times Adrienne got Rick to go down to the chapel with her. He played the keyboard while they sang together, the way they use too. There was a minister at the hospital. It was the minister's job to visit the patient's room to encourage and pray for them. It was setup to where the patients, their family members, the hospital staff or whomsoever could go to the worship service area in the hospital. They had different ministers that worked in the hospital to come in to preach and pray with those that choose to be prayed for and go into the house of the Lord for a word of encouragement. After the minister came into Rick's room for the second time in the time he was in the hospital. Rick began accusing Adrienne of the minister the reason why he was coming into his room was to see her. Adrienne tried to explain to Rick that that was the minister's job there at the hospital to visit the sick and pray for them. Adrienne was embarrassed that Rick would act that way with a man of God. That took time out to come and pray for him and he acted as though the man wasn't even there. Adrienne wanted to believe it was the side effects of his treatments. She didn't know who Rick was anymore. It was like he had turned his back on God and Adrienne. Adrienne was getting sick herself just being at the hospital with him. Rick kept it so hot in the room, it wasn't cool enough to keep down the germs and Adrienne was having flu like symptoms to the point she had to wear a mask. Adrienne decided to turn the air up after Rick had fallen off to sleep. One of the nurses came in the room and woke Rick up, he asked the nurse what the temperature was on. The nurse told him what it was on. Rick asked her to turn the temperature down. Once again Adrienne tried to explain to him that the room needed to be cooler to keep down germs, but he wasn't hearing it. The room had gotten so stuffy Adrienne couldn't sleep. So she told Rick she was going to go home and she would be back after church the next day. Rick called security on Adrienne so she wouldn't leave the hospital in his truck. When security approached Adrienne, she had made it outside of the hospital. Two security officers escorted her back up to Rick's room. One of the officers asked Adrienne what was going on? Adrienne explained, to the officer about the room being so hot the heat would hit you in the face when she walked in the room. When the officers walked in the room, they realized what Adrienne was talking about. Rick had told the officers, he didn't want Adrienne to leave in his truck. One of the officers said to Adrienne. Ma'am if he don't want you to leave in his truck, then you can't leave in his truck. Adrienne said to the officer, she wasn't going to be able to stay in the room, it was making her sick. Rick said to the officer, he wanted the temperature in the room to be the same when he got out from under the covers as it was under the covers. The officer realized what Rick was saying and told Adrienne she could go on home. Because Rick had pajamas he could have put on but he choose to lay there in his shorts and a T-shirt. Flirting with the nurses was what he was doing the reason he didn't want to put on his pajamas. When Adrienne returned to the hospital, one of the nurses had drawn a tongue hanging out of the mouth on the board where she was suppose to sign her name. That let Adrienne know he was flirting with the nurses. The nurses continued to flirt back with him right to Adrienne's face as though she wasn't even there. Rick was released from the hospital and the first place he wanted to stop was his ex-wife house. He said, he wanted to see his grandchildren, but he had an excuse to go to his ex-wife house everyday. Adrienne said to Rick, he didn't need to be around people for a few days after his treatment. But Rick wasn't hearing it. Adrienne decided she would drive straight home. If he wanted to go to his ex-wife house, he was going to drive himself there. Adrienne got out of the truck and didn't look back because she couldn't tell him anything. He did what he wanted to do. The next two days Niece called Adrienne telling her she had to take Rick back to the hospital. He had setup an infection. Niece was there to help Rick spend his money but she wanted Adrienne to be there for him.

Rick had his own house and Adrienne had her own house before they were married. The Lord blessed Adrienne to pay off her house years before she and Rick married. Rick's house wasn't. They visited each other back and forth. Whenever Adrienne visited Rick's house, they would be sitting on the couch watching a movie, and all of a sudden the door opened. It was Niece, she didn't bother to knock or anything. She had no respect to the fact that Adrienne was there. Adrienne wasn't use to person just walking up in the house without knocking, but with Rick it didn't seem to matter to him. He did the same thing when he came to Adrienne's house even though he had a key. But that still didn't give him the right to just walk up in her house Adrienne thought. She had to ask him to ring the doorbell to let her know he was there. Because sometime she would be in the shower when he came, and when she got out of the shower he would be peeping around the corner trying to scare her instead of letting her know he was there. Adrienne asked, Rick one day why was it Niece didn't knock before coming into the house? And all Rick had to say was, I don't know. Adrienne thought she have never just walked into her dad's house, especially if she didn't live their. Adrienne could tell Niece was spoiled. God said, to train up a child in the way they should go so when they are old, they want depart from it. When we spare the rod, we spoil the child, and Rick chose to spoil the child. Adrienne never had that problem with her children just walking into her house without knocking, rather they had a key, or not. It was all about respect, they always called to let Adrienne know they were coming over, and then knocked or rang the door when they got there. But it seemed that Rick had no problem with whatever Niece did. It got to the point where Adrienne just stopped asking him anything about Niece. Rick didn't want Adrienne to ask him anything about Niece. He would get so angry. Rick and Niece drove around switching vehicles back and forth as though the two of them were married. The way Adrienne and Rick should have been doing. Rick thought he could still do what he wanted to do even after he got married. It bothered Adrienne that Rick thought it was alright for Niece and his ex-wife to ride around in his vehicles which everything was suppose to be his' and Adrienne together after they married. But Adrienne had no say so in nothing he did without him getting angry with her. But he was the one in the wrong. One night Rick and Adrienne were on their way to church to a revival. They stopped by Rick's house to pick up his tie he had left there. And to Adrienne's surprise, there was Rick's ex-wife car parked under the car porch as though she lived there. When Adrienne asked him what her car was doing there? He said to her that Niece and her mother had to go somewhere. Adrienne wondered why was his ex-wife riding around in his car? Once again, he didn't see anything wrong with it. He thought Adrienne was suppose to except what ever they did and go on. Adrienne said to Rick, she didn't think his ex-wife should be riding around in his vehicle. Adrienne didn't like what he was doing to her. But he played it off as if nothing was wrong. He thought if he kept her high, she wouldn't have anything to say about what he was doing. But it didn't work. Adrienne asked God to take smoking marijuana away from her just like she asked Him to take smoking cigarettes away from her. Every time Adrienne tried to smoke a joint it would sting her throat making it easy for her to stop, thank God. Out of love and respect for Rick, Adrienne pretended that it didn't bother her. She prayed that this too would pass and love over comes evil any day. Adrienne realized she was being lead in the wrong direction when she read in the Bible that her ways were not God's ways and God's ways were not her ways. She knew she had to get back on the right path. Adrienne said to Rick, she wasn't going to smoke marijuana anymore. She asked him to stop and he pretended that he had. But he hid it from her until she found half a joint in the truck one day he came to take her to the doctor. Adrienne decided to put Rick in God's hands. She knew God could fix it better then she could. Adrienne prayed for God to lead and guide her husband everyday. But the more she prayed things got worse instead of better. Rick couldn't see the fact that Niece didn't want the two of them together. Adrienne felt that Niece was hoping Rick would get back with her mom. Rick had given Adrienne a key to his house. When Niece found out Adrienne had a key to the door she changed the locks. Adrienne asked Rick why Niece changed the locks? He said, he didn't know. The day Rick told Adrienne he couldn't take care of her really hurt her. He wanted the sex part of the marriage, but he didn't want the responsibility that went along with the marriage. Adrienne had to apply for food stamps it was so embarrassing that she had a husband making good money and he choose not to support her. That hurt her more then the pain she was experiencing in her body. For a man to tell his wife he couldn't take care of her, Adrienne realized that was not of God. She found herself in a real jam. She had no income, her car had put her down. She had to walk and pick up cans along the road just to pay a bill. She thanked God that she was debt free. She only had utility bills to pay. It was hard for her having to ask her daughter Audrey to help her sometime to pay her utility bills. Rick started out giving her fifty sometime seventy—five dollars a week. But as time went on he stopped giving her anything at all. Adrienne thought about the man Jesus told to sale all he had and Follow Him. So Adrienne sold all the gold jewelry she had and stepped out on faith asking God to help her budget the money she received. She even paid her tithes out of the money. She didn't get nearly what it was worth but something was better then nothing. There were times God made a way out of no way for her. Rick said, he had been divorced for the past eighteen years when they got together. Adrienne wondered why he never remarried after all that time? She found out the hard way why? She realized it was Rick's daughter and ex-wife that had a lost to do with him not doing anything for Adrienne. Adrienne wished she had never married him. She didn't think Rick knew how to say no to other people. But he had no problem saying no to her. He continued right on putting Niece, her mother and his grandchildren before Adrienne. She was last in everything. But Adrienne decided to give that over to God too. The most time they spend together under one roof was when Rick was in the hospital. Adrienne still gave God praise in songs through it all. She loved Rick, but hated his ways. Everything had to be his way. Adrienne tried to sanctify Rick in God's way, but he refused to hear her. He had an excuse for everything. Things weren't going the way Adrienne thought they should with her living in one place and Rick in another. But he was where he wanted to be which was where his daughter and grand kids were.

For the first five years Rick was Adrienne's supplier of marijuana. She smoked it trying to numb the pain, hoping it would help her cope with the pain of what Rick was putting her through. And the way people were treating her every where she turned in the church and her family members. The devil was determined to destroy her. Adrienne never had much to say to people. She thought, that was why she was treated so badly. From a child Adrienne didn't have the strength to stand up for herself. But she continued to treat people the way she wanted to be treated. She watched how other people acted, and took whatever they threw at her. As she continued to study the bible she realized it wasn't her people hated and mistreated, but it was the God in her that they hated. Adrienne thought smoking marijuana would help her keep her mind off of her problems, but it didn't. She felt no one cared what she was going through. But she felt too embarrassed to tell anyone what she was going through. She didn't understand herself what was going on with her. She walked around most of the time in a daze. Adrienne was having problems with the side effects of the medication. Adrienne taught Sunday school to the young children which she enjoyed doing very much. And at the same time she was teaching herself the ways of God. God opened Adrienne's eyes one day to the truth and it got her thinking. She wondered how could she be teaching the word of God and doing wrong herself smoking marijuana? She thanked God, for blessing her with another chance. She realized she could have been dead and gone. Adrienne repented asking God to forgive her of her sins knowingly and unknowingly. God delivered her from smoking marijuana, fornication, and cigarettes. Seeing all that the Lord had done for her and brought her through, strengthened her faith in God. And she asked God to deliver her from everything that was not like Him. She realized that it was God and His Son Jesus that she needed all alone. God said, to seek ye first the kingdom of God, and all of His righteousness and everything else will be added unto you. Adrienne realized it was time that she did something to please God and not man. She made a vow to God that she would go if she had to go by herself. She gave that pain of hurt and anger over to God as she sang His Praises and witnessed to the goodness of God. Like the woman at the well, Adrienne had five husbands, they were not men chosen by God but of her own doing. None of them did right by her. Adrienne realized she was trying to do things on her own. No knowing she needed to trust in God in every area of her life. It wasn't until she learned to trust in God that her life changed for the better. Adrienne learned to Pray, stand still and see the salvation of the Lord. God said, that we not be unequally yoked, one person going in one direction and the other person in another direction, cause it want work. It is better to obey God then man. Man do things there own way instead of the way God said to do. Adrienne thought about all the time she had wasted with men that didn't appreciate the God in her. What the devil mint for her bad, God turned it around for her good. She finally realized she was trying to do everything herself. But with God all things are possible, without Him we are doomed. My Lord and Savior Jesus Christ, I love Him. It wasn't easy the more Adrienne strive to obey God the worse her situation became. She realized, by this time the devil was trying to block her progress. Using whomever he could to try and turn her away from God. But her God had the last say so. Adrienne learned how to give God all the glory, honor, and praise for keeping her in her right mind. There were times Adrienne thought she was going to lose her mind. But God stepped in right on time.

Adrienne realized she was doing better before she and Rick were married. Things got worse afterward. She knew God honored marriages, but you have to be careful whom you marry. Especially when they are not following after Christ. Adrienne realized she was being lead in the wrong direction when she asked God to deliver her from smoking marijuana. She wanted to stop hurting herself so she decided to stop following and watching Rick flirting with other women as though she wasn't there. The day of Adrienne and Rick's marriage, Adrienne's two daughters showed up to witness the marriage. But Rick's daughter was no where to be found. She didn't know if Rick even told her they were getting married. Rick showed up at the courthouse in his work clothes as if it didn't matter if they got married or not. Then he went on back to work after the vows were exchanged. Adrienne went home and waited for her husband arrival later that night. As they retired to the bedroom for the night, Niece called right as they were making love. It was ten o'clock at night and Adrienne didn't answer the phone after ten unless it was an emergency. She would let the answering machine answer that time of night. Rick heard that the voice on the answering machine was Niece. He stopped making love to answer the phone. Adrienne thought he could have waited, and called her back afterwards. The next night she called again same time. The third night she called again same time. It was as if Niece had a mirror looking at them as they got in position to make love. She wanted her dad to come back home and be with her. So out of curiosity Adrienne decided to ask Rick why it was that Niece waited so late to call every night? What did she do that for? The devil came out in him. His attitude changed that night causing an argument to get started. He shouted at Adrienne telling her what she had better do whenever his daughter called. While he pushed Adrienne to the floor. Adrienne knew right then Rick and Niece was going to be a problem. Adrienne had been though enough in her life to know that he was not going to talk to her any kind of way. Not in her own house. She was already having problems with pain in her body and for him to push her down. That was unexpected. Adrienne thought she should have called the police on him, but she made up in her mind that night if she had to fight him then she didn't need him. She asked him to leave that night to go and be with his daughter and he wasted no time doing just that. Adrienne then realized his daughter was the reason he never remarried. She came between every woman he every dated. It was as if he was looking for a reason to go back and be with her. He gathered what stuff he had at the house and moved back to his house to be with his daughter. It wouldn't be so bad if she was a child but this was a grown woman. Adrienne had gotten tied of the games they were playing anyway. Adrienne had to see Rick at church on Sunday morning and he acted as if nothing happened. She respected him in the Lord's house and as her husband, but the problem was still there. After God her husband was the one person she thought she could count on the most. But he turned out to be a disappointment to her. He never apologized to Adrienne for anything he did. Adrienne was always the apologetic one even when she was right. He was to busy doing for everybody else and didn't have time for her. He couldn't see that she needed for him to be her husband for real. There were things needing to be done around the house that Adrienne couldn't do and she needed his help to do them like mowing the lawn. But he was so wrapped up in Niece and his music he acted just like he didn't have a wife. Whenever she needed his help with something his words were he don't have time. Adrienne was so tied of hearing him say those words that it wasn't funny. She had to give him sex to get him to do anything for her and sometime then he still didn't have time. He would break or tear up more then he fixed. Adrienne said, he would do it on purpose so she wouldn't ask him to do anything else. Rick had a mean strike in him he tried to hide but he showed to Adrienne on several occasions. She realized later on that it wasn't that he didn't have time to do anything but he really didn't know how to do much of anything unless it was something he wanted to do. Rick was always in a hurry the same way Adrienne had been in the pass. He was clumsy as well. They remained friends, at least Adrienne still considered him to be a friend through it all, because she realized it wasn't Rick but that evil spirit controlling him. Adrienne knew she had to be a doer of God's word not just a hearer only. God said, to love those that despite fully misuse you. So Adrienne continued to love Rick despite the way he treated her. She continued to strive to be like Christ, in order to be a servant of the Lord.

Adrienne was always an independent person. She had to be, growing up the way she did. If she saw something that needed to be done she just did it without being asked or told to do it. She knew that God didn't make any mistakes. But she was really sad after her mother passed away, things were happening faster then she was able to comprehend. She didn't get to know much about her before she died. It was like a dream. Adrienne couldn't understand the reason for the abuse of other people. She was paralysis with fear that made her angry inside. But she could never act on that anger. The thought that people could be so mean for no reason at all. She had no idea how to handle her situation. She wanted to hurt them back but she didn't have it in her to hurt anyone. She showed love but got hatred in return. For years she tried to block it all out of her mind. But she saw nothing but disappointment was all around her. She had no knowledge of God, nor did she understand why she was here on this earth or how she got here. Terrible things kept happening to her, the more she tried, evil was present to knock her down further. Other people around her seem to be happy and acting like everything was right with them. But Adrienne knew something wasn't right with her, and she had no one to talk to about it. Her grandmother lived not far down the road but she wasn't aloud to leave from the house unless she was going to school or church. Adrienne went through life trying to love everyone but they were out to hurt her using her for what they could get from her. Although she was good person that wasn't good enough just to be a good person. God knows her heart ached with sadness on the inside. But she was still willing to do for others no matter how they treated her. It was as if nothing she did was ever good enough. But she realized what the devil meant for her bad, God turned it around for her good.

As a little girl, Adrienne could see a big hog hanging from a tree. It was so big that the limb broke, there were little baby pigs running around wanting to be feed. There was a out house during the day, and a pot to use at night for the bathroom. They had to pick cotton over across the railroad tracks, someone tried to put Adrienne upon a big white horse, but she was so little, and the horse was so big. She was afraid of the horse and started to cry. That life to her was heaven compared to the hell she had been going through since her mother died. Adrienne felt so all a lone after she died. Everything went wrong from there, she grew up in an abusive household. Picked on all the time at home and school. Being blamed for other people wrong doings because she was too afraid to stand up for herself. Hanna hated Adrienne so she had no one to teach her things she needed to know as a young lady. She suffered a lot because of her fears. Ending up in one abusive marriage or relationship after the other, trying to do what she thought in her heart to be right. But after becoming saved, sanctified and filled with the Holy Ghost Adrienne realized that her ways were not the ways of God. Obedience is better then sacrifice, and she sacrificed a lot of herself over the years due to ignorance on her part. God blessed her down through the years with little to no income. But God made a way out no way. All of her bills got paid, only once did her lights get turned off in those seventeen years. Adrienne was too sick to get up and go pay the bill. The devil thought if she didn't have a vehicle she couldn't go to church and receive the word of God. But to God be the Glory, her pastor and first lady would take time of their busy schedule after traveling so far from home to pick her up on Sunday morning and bible study. If the pastor couldn't make it or was going to be late, he or the first lady would call one of the other church members to make sure she had a way to church, praise God. Niece stole Adrienne's vehicle out of her yard in the middle of the night. After Adrienne had paid the vehicle off. Niece didn't want the vehicle before it was paid off. But God is so good that He blessed Adrienne in five months time was blessed with another vehicle better then the one that was stolen. Adrienne realized just how good God is. He is a merciful and forgiving God. God carried Adrienne through so much in her life that she just couldn't thank Him enough, nor could she tell it all. There were times she wanted to give up, but God had a purpose for her life. Adrienne promised the Lord that she would serve Him until He called her home. She realized she had been blind, but know could see. She thought, of Job after all he went through, he said to God. Though you slay me, yet will I trust you, he still trusted in God. That was Adrienne's prayer each and every day to God. Though you slay me yet will I trust you. Adrienne was like the woman with the issue of blood for seventeen years. She went from doctor to doctor spending all of her money. She met a man name Jesus and was healed. Studying the Bible everyday helped Adrienne to understand that it wasn't a earthly man she need, but it was Jesus all alone. Her soul looked back and wondered how she got over counting it all joy. Keeping the faith as she continued giving God Praise. She has been redeemed and welcomed into God's family. Still giving God the Praise for His Amazing Grace. Hallelujah!

P.S. Not being rooted and grounded in the word of God makes it so easy to be deceived by the devil.

Finished product: June 11, 2012
Copyright: July 15, 2015

Printed in the United States
By Bookmasters